PRAISE FOR *THE GREATEST YOU*

"Trent Shelton's message of hope, betterment, and self-love reaches hearts worldwide, inspiring us to never give up. Trent's *The Greatest You* dives deeper to show us that the real obstacles are our choices and he teaches us how to conquer our struggles daily to become better."
—John C. Maxwell, author and motivational speaker

"Trent Shelton is one of the most authentic and powerful voices in personal development today. In *The Greatest You* he uses real-life truth telling to take readers on a deeper dive into how they can become a better version of themselves, and he provides the tactical steps to let go of behaviors that no longer serve them. If you want to become the best you, but are unsure how to get there, start here."
—Rachel Hollis, #1 *New York Times* bestselling author
of *Girl, Wash Your Face* and *Girl, Stop Apologizing*

"If you've ever struggled to deal with your past or find your true purpose, then *The Greatest You* is going to change your life. Trent Shelton—one of the most inspiring teachers alive today—has written a playbook for letting go of the pain, protecting your peace, creating great relationships, and growing into your best self. I loved every page."
—Brendon Burchard, #1 *New York Times* bestselling author
of *High Performance Habits* and *The Motivation Manifesto*

"With so much noise and distraction in today's crazy-busy world, you need a voice that stands out, reaches into your soul, and gives you the answers and the tools to overcome your challenges and achieve more. Trent Shelton is that voice and with his heart of gold, he created the must-read book of the year. Don't think, just read!"
—Dean Graziosi, multiple *New York Times* bestselling author,
including the #1 bestseller *Millionaire Success Habits*

THE GREATEST YOU

FACE REALITY, RELEASE NEGATIVITY, AND LIVE YOUR PURPOSE

Trent Shelton with Lou Aronica

NELSON
BOOKS

An Imprint of Thomas Nelson

Published in Nashville, Tennessee, by Nelson Books, an imprint of Thomas Nelson. Nelson Books and Thomas Nelson are registered trademarks of HarperCollins Christian Publishing, Inc.

Rehabbers' names have been changed and identifying details masked.

Thomas Nelson titles may be purchased in bulk for educational, business, fund-raising, or sales promotional use. For information, please e-mail SpecialMarkets@ThomasNelson.com.

Scripture quotations are taken from the Holy Bible, New International Version®, NIV®. Copyright © 1973, 1978, 1984, 2011 by Biblica, Inc.® Used by permission of Zondervan. All rights reserved worldwide. www.Zondervan.com. The "NIV" and "New International Version" are trademarks registered in the United States Patent and Trademark Office by Biblica, Inc.®

Any Internet addresses, phone numbers, or company or product information printed in this book are offered as a resource and are not intended in any way to be or to imply an endorsement by Thomas Nelson, nor does Thomas Nelson vouch for the existence, content, or services of these sites, phone numbers, companies, or products beyond the life of this book.

ISBN 978-1-4002-0793-0 (HC)
ISBN 978-1-4002-0794-7 (eBook)

Library of Congress Control Number: 2018964373

Printed in the United States of America
19 20 21 22 23 LSC 10 9 8 7 6 5 4 3

I would like to dedicate this book to all the Rehabbers across the world. Without your support, I would never have found the strength to turn my pain into my power. I thank God every day for all of you. Let's get it!

CONTENTS

INTRODUCTION

Ten years ago, I couldn't even remotely imagine that more than nine million people would view my latest video, share it more than two hundred thousand times, and make more than fifteen thousand often very personal comments. If you'd told me that I'd have six million people following me on Facebook, a million on Instagram, and an overall social media reach of fifty million, I would have said you were tripping. Back then, if someone had suggested that I would be considered one of the most inspiring people on the web and one of the biggest influences on positivity in this generation, I would have said that this person had in mind a different Trent Shelton. Because the Trent Shelton of ten years ago was super-introverted. He had a fear of public speaking and no experience with it. He also had tattoos all over his body, so he sure didn't look the part of an inspirational speaker.

And the truth is, it couldn't have been me, because I wasn't *ready* for it to be me. Don't get me wrong; I knew that I wanted to help people, and I knew that reaching out to others filled me with a sense of purpose. But there was something I had to do first.

I had to get my own life together.

I had to do the work that I'm going to share with you in this book.

Ten years ago, I was in a terrible place in both my professional and personal lives. I'm going to get into this in detail in chapter 1, but for now let me just say that it felt as though I was losing every battle. I wasn't helping myself, and I sure wasn't helping anyone else.

Then, seemingly out of nowhere, I got an offer from a friend to speak in front of five thousand teenagers at his church. Public speaking was not my thing, and I worried that this was going to be just the latest in a series of disasters for me. But it was on that stage that I unlocked something in me, something I'd had deep inside all along—my true purpose. I almost blew it because, even though I'd prepared ridiculously hard, when I stepped onto the stage, I just *went blank*. So right then, when panic could have leveled me, I just started talking in what would become my straight-up, straight-from-the-heart, no-filter speaking style. I had no notes to lean on—just my truth and my experiences. Kids know what's real, so I had to be real, and they really felt what I was saying and couldn't stop asking me questions afterward. It was then that I realized a very important lesson about life: you don't have to be perfect to help people; all you have to do is be real. The kids repeatedly told me how much they respected me, not just because they were inspired, but because they finally felt understood. Those kids made me realize the power of transparency. My being honest about my life gave them the confidence to be honest about their own. I promised myself that I would always speak this way in the future. It felt incredible to witness how my transparency was the first step to their transformation. Affecting their lives made me feel alive again. It was the first time I actually felt a purpose outside of football, and what really tripped me out was how natural it felt to inspire those kids.

I knew this was the first step in rehabbing my own life. If I was going to preach it, I had to practice it. If I was going to talk it, I had to live it. Becoming the greatest me became my mission, and I dedicated myself to becoming nothing less. The responsibility I had to others—most importantly, my young son, Tristan—gave me an entirely new level of motivation. Taking my life to the next level was no longer an option; it was a must. I knew Tristan was going to follow my lead, so I had to give him a model that would put his life on the best possible path. And as I continued to work on myself, I started tweeting about it with the hashtag #RehabTime, recording my transformation through two-minute videos under the same name. I thought RehabTime was just for me, but I quickly realized it was bigger than me. *Much bigger than me.*

As RehabTime began to connect with people, I started interacting with my followers. The most unforgettable of these experiences was with Ashley, an encounter that showed me why God created me. It wasn't for football, as I'd thought up to that point; it was for RehabTime. I met Ashley at an event, and she told me that not that long before, she'd been so ready to end her life that she had a gun in her hand, cocked and loaded. Her mind was made up, and nothing was going to change it. She was going on Facebook to say her goodbyes.

Her plan was to press Post and then kill herself. But when she got on Facebook, a video popped up that I'd made at two o'clock that very morning. Something had woken me out of my sleep to make it, which I now realize was God telling me to get this message to Ashley. The video was titled "Don't End Your Life," and in it, I urged people to fight through, to just give tomorrow a chance. Storms suck, but storms don't last forever. Ashley watched that video, and instead of killing herself, she wrote a positive Facebook message about her life and what she was dealing with. Her message helped others dealing with suicidal thoughts that night. While she thought she was alone in her struggle, she wasn't. At that moment she understood there was a purpose greater than her pain, and the most painful moment of her life became her most purposeful one.

At another early event, two teenagers came up, hugged me, and started crying. They told me that I had helped save their mother's life. Even though I didn't want to take the credit, they insisted that if it hadn't been for my video, they would be motherless. She was fighting drug addiction, and an overdose seemed to be in her near future. But she watched one of my videos, which sparked a change and encouraged her to face her reality. She realized that it was time to go to war and overcome her addiction—not just for herself, but also for her children.

The videos and speaking engagements were definitely helping people, but the desperation out there was bigger than I ever imagined—millions and millions of people were convinced their lives were worthless, that they were stuck in a hole they could never climb out of, that their stories were over. These people needed to discover what I'd discovered for myself—that even though your story may have some bad chapters in it, it can still end well.

But let's be real: it's almost impossible to conquer your struggles alone. Everyone needs help, but the kind of help you get makes a big difference. You don't need someone at the mountaintop, telling you how to get up there. You need someone next to you, climbing the mountain with you. Someone to give you the tools to overcome your pain. Someone speaking to your heart and urging you to never stop climbing.

That's where this book comes in.

When your life is a serious mess, you don't need someone to offer you a bunch of empty advice. You need someone who is going to be by your side as you work your way out of it. You need someone to say, "I understand where you're at, I'm here for you, and we will conquer this together." My videos get a ton of views, which is great, but what I love the most is how much interaction they create. When more than a hundred thousand people feel so connected to what I'm saying on a video that they respond in a deeply personal way, I know they understand that I'm on their side, that we're fighting this battle as teammates. They understand that I'm not giving up on them, and they don't need to give up on themselves. I'm not trying to be an oracle; I'm trying to be a colleague, a supporter, a friend. I call my followers; I respond to their messages; I even send some of them personal encouragement videos. This is all very real for me, because I understand the consequences of desperation.

So, this book is a promise. You want to take your life to a better place? I'll be there with you, inspiring you to become your greatest you. Are you ready to do the work necessary to become the best version of yourself? If so, I offer you the benefit of my experience and the experiences of others who have been so generous to share their stories with me. I'll be there, coaching you up and giving you the tools you need to get out of a bad situation and on to something so much better.

There's hard work coming in this book. You're going to have to face some things that maybe you'd prefer not to face. You're going to have to get rid of some things in your life that are going to be very hard to get rid of. But I'll stick with you, every step of the way, sharing with you how I dealt with *the same situations*.

Throughout this book, I'll be sharing parts of my personal journey and showing the lessons these experiences have taught me. I will also share lots and lots of stories from followers all over the globe—people who have gone through (and might still be going through) hard times and feel that their stories might offer others something to identify with and provide a sense of comfort. I've changed their names here for their own protection, but I promise you these stories are as real as they are raw.

Enough introduction. We have work to do.

Are you ready to become the greatest you? Then it's RehabTime.

Let's get it.

1

YOU'LL NEVER WIN YOUR WAR BY RUNNING FROM YOUR BATTLES

Let's get right into this. Listen: If this book is going to work for you, you're going to have to be real with yourself. And if I'm going to ask you to be real with yourself, the least I can do is start the process with some transparency of my own.

Ten years ago I was in a very dark place. My life was all about football, though the challenges in my life certainly didn't end there. From the time I was a kid, I was always one of the best players on the field. I remember the first three times I ever touched a football; all three plays went for touchdowns. Before I was even a teenager, there was no doubt in my mind that I was destined to play on Sundays in the NFL.

My future seemed even more certain when I starred as a wide receiver for Baylor University. I was ready for a long career in the league. When Draft Day came around, I watched every pick of the draft. Experts had told me that I was likely to go in the later rounds, but it was possible I could go higher, so I stayed glued to ESPN from the start, waiting to hear my name called.

Except it never was. Two days. Seven rounds. Two hundred fifty-five players, thirty-four of them wide receivers, like I was—and not one of them was me. I'd be lying if I said that didn't hurt. It did. But I had to hide my hurt behind a smile. I had to pretend I wasn't worried that my lifelong dream wouldn't be coming true.

Fifteen minutes after the draft, my worry started to fade, as multiple teams called, trying to sign me as a high-priority free agent. After getting counsel from my uncle George Stewart (who has been coaching in the NFL for more than twenty years), I decided to sign with the Indianapolis Colts. They were fresh off a Super Bowl title, and I knew I had the skills to help them get another ring. I just knew Peyton Manning and I were going to be making big plays all over the field. I just knew it.

I got to training camp, and things were going great. I started at the bottom of the totem pole because I wasn't a returning player or a high draft pick, but I got off to a great start in the preseason, maybe the best in the NFL, and certainly the best among rookies. Undrafted free agents are always a long shot to make the team, but I was turning heads; I was balling out, and I was sure I was going to make the squad.

Then the Colts didn't play me in the third preseason game. That didn't make sense to me because I'd been playing so well. I asked some of the veteran players about it, and they told me that the team was trying to hide me because they didn't want other teams signing me. That didn't make one bit of sense to me; doing that would only make sense if *they* weren't planning to sign me. And in spite of how well I'd played, that's exactly what happened. They cut me and then re-signed me to the practice squad, which meant I wouldn't suit up for games but could still get a call at some point. I figured I'd be in Indianapolis for the whole season, so I got an apartment and a car. Then, after week two, they cut me from the practice squad. All of a sudden, I'd gone from visions of being an NFL star to being right back in my room in my parents' house, not wanting to go out because I was too embarrassed to talk to anyone about what had happened to me. Not getting drafted hurt, but this hurt even more. I'd been working for this since I was six years old. How could it be slipping away from me?

A week later, I was back on the practice squad, and a few weeks after that, Coach Tony Dungy told me I was going to be moved to the active roster for a Monday night game against the San Diego Chargers. *Okay,* I thought, *this didn't start out the way I wanted, but everything is turning around for me. Ten years from now, my friends and I will laugh about how I was worried that my long NFL career wasn't going to happen.*

But something wasn't right with my knee. I'd been feeling it for a while, and I ignored it because I had to; I couldn't afford to let an injury get in my way. The problem was that it wasn't getting any better. I had to pop a pain pill before every practice just to get on the field. I knew that if I sat out of practice, I would be going home. No team needs an injured guy on the practice squad, and they certainly don't need an unproven guy that isn't 100 percent healthy on the active roster. I tried to fight through it, but Coach saw me limping and he told me that the team couldn't afford to activate me if I wasn't able to go full speed. I knew in that moment that I had lost out on a huge opportunity. I stayed on the practice squad the rest of the year, but I never got another chance to get into a game.

The next season, I was invited to minicamp with the Seattle Seahawks. They wound up cutting me right at the end of preseason, but then a week later they called and said they wanted me to come back—that very day, in fact. I quickly packed some things, rushed off to the airport, and was just about to board my plane when I got another call from Seattle. They'd changed their minds.

I got one more shot with the Washington Redskins. I was completely healthy, and I ran the fastest time of my life—a 4.3-second 40-yard dash, which is superfast. The Redskins signed me to the practice squad, but I never got any further, even though I had great practices. By November, they had cut me and I'd learned firsthand the real meaning of the initials NFL: *not for long*.

I refused to believe that my dream was over. I just kept running from reality, because reality didn't connect with the vision I had for myself. I was a football player—it was the only way I knew to define myself—so I had to keep running from the fact that football wasn't happening for me.

If the NFL didn't want me—yet—there were other options. There was the Arena Football League, and they were happy to have me. The game was brutal on my body because the fields are small and the turf is laid over concrete, but at least I was playing. Then I got a call from my college coach to come play for the United Football League, a new professional league that had been trying to compete directly with the NFL. I had a great tryout and ran one of my fastest forties ever. They said they were going to sign me, and I thought this could be my ticket to the pros. Two weeks later, I got a call saying the league was going to fold. It had lost too much money, and football fans had made it clear they didn't want a new league.

Reality had gotten right up in my face, but still I kept running. I was fast during tryouts, but I was even faster when I was running away from the truth. And while I was running, I was doing all kinds of other destructive things to my life. I started smoking and drinking, and I was partying all the time. I was running around with women even though I had an on-again, off-again girlfriend I'd met when I was with the Colts. I didn't care about life. I was living reckless. I was doing anything and everything to fill me up inside, because I was feeling awfully empty in there. Living reckless meant that I didn't have to face up to what was really happening. And I thought I could keep this going indefinitely.

Then I got a woman who wasn't my girlfriend pregnant. I wasn't ready in any way to have a kid, and I made this very, very clear. Maria made it equally clear that she was keeping the baby, which freaked me out. Meanwhile, I had to tell my girlfriend (we were on again, sort of) that I'd gotten another woman pregnant. You can imagine how that went. Complicating the fact was that my mother and my girlfriend's mother were close friends, and this had created a huge amount of friction between them. I was a jerk at the time because I didn't want to be a man, but I was blaming everyone else. I just wanted to keep running.

And then I couldn't run any longer. I got a call telling me that my college roommate, Anthony Arline, had committed suicide. He had made the Chargers but then had to leave for personal reasons, and the loss of his football dreams had a big effect on him, ultimately causing him to take his own life.

I was devastated, because Anthony was one of my closest friends. And I was even more devastated because I hadn't been paying enough attention to see what he was going through. Maybe if I had, I could have convinced him to keep going. Maybe I could have helped him see a way out.

That was rock bottom for me. That was when I realized that I had to face up to my reality. It was at Anthony's funeral that I finally understood that life isn't promised, that we aren't guaranteed tomorrow. If I wanted to leave a mark on the world, I was going to have to start working toward that. I had to do it for my newborn son. I had to do it for Anthony. I had to do it for all the people like Anthony who might still be able to make their lives work. By this time I had started RehabTime and released a few videos, but this was when I really decided to dedicate myself to helping people. Back then, I only had a few thousand Facebook followers, and I would open my phone line up at night to them, saying that if they were going through a tough time, they should call. And here's something I never would have imagined: doing this felt better than professional football had ever felt to me. When I was helping people, I felt that I was truly living my purpose, and if I was really being honest with myself, I didn't have a love for the game anymore. Football wasn't quite in my rearview mirror yet, but it was almost there. The most important thing was that I'd stopped running. I finally realized that I couldn't win this war if I kept running from my battles, and this was a war I absolutely needed to win, not just for me but for everyone around me.

Preparing for Battle

Look: you and I both know that the truth can be very scary. Sometimes it's just much easier to live with a difficult situation, one that is slowly draining us of everything we're made of, than to see things exactly as they are and commit to doing the work to get out of that situation. That's exactly what I was doing when I was bouncing from practice squads to arena football to leagues that never got off the ground. Rather than face the reality that was forcing itself on me, I ran from my battle. This was something I didn't want to see, couldn't let myself see. If I acknowledged that my football life was over, I was afraid that I wouldn't have a life at all, because my significance, my identity, and my confidence were all wrapped up in football. Without football, who would I be?

I was putting my life on hold to pursue a passion I no longer actually felt. And this was turning me angry and dark. But the truth was—and this is true for all of us—no matter how fast I ran, my reality was never going to get farther away. Your reality *always* keeps pace with you. Even while I was in the middle of this turmoil, I had some idea that running wasn't going to help. But I was so afraid of acknowledging that my football career was over that I convinced myself it was better to keep running. And I kept thinking about some practical issues: How was I going to provide for my new family if I didn't have football as a source of income? Looking back now, I can see that I was just delaying my healing, delaying my purpose, delaying my true identity. At the time, though, running truly felt to me like the only choice, but my life had become a complete mess because of it, and it was affecting everything and everyone around me.

Anthony was dead and my son was nearly two, and that's when I finally realized that doing what I was doing wasn't okay anymore. My son was one of the few bright lights in my life, and I had to face up to my situation if I was going to create a good future for him. I couldn't let him get trapped in my darkness.

So, from that place, I allowed myself to look at the situation as it really was. I was never going to play football at the top level again, and if that was the case, I needed to find my true self. I'm not going to tell you this didn't hurt—it did. Bad. But it was a temporary hurt, and until I allowed myself to feel it, I couldn't go on to be the person God intended me to be.

So, yeah, I understand why people run from their battles; I truly do. But here's the problem. If you feel that things aren't right in your life, if you feel that your situation is getting a little bit worse all the time, if you feel that just getting up in the morning is becoming a struggle because it means you've got to live with your circumstances, then you really only have one of two choices: You can sink or you can swim. You can let things keep getting more and more miserable—or you can go to war. But if you're going to go to war, then running from your battles is no longer an option. Yes, you might survive if you keep running, but how is that kind of survival working out for you? It's time to stand and fight, and the first thing you have to do is understand what you're fighting and why. You have to come face-to-face with your reality.

Why do so many of us run from our reality? It's because there are so many roadblocks preventing us from getting to our goal of a more satisfying and more fulfilled life. These roadblocks come in many varieties, but there are four I hear from people all the time:

1. **Addictions.** Most of us have some sort of addiction that we're battling in some way. It may not necessarily be one of the "big" ones, like drugs, alcohol, and sex, but other addictions can be just as troublesome. Maybe you're addicted to sugar. Maybe you're addicted to work. Maybe you're addicted to social media or unhealthy relationships. Whatever your addiction, it is an enormous roadblock in your life and an impediment to facing up to your reality. The truth is that addictions are a way of escaping reality, and yet, their very existence interferes with you reaching your goals. Now, obviously, if addictions were easy to break, they wouldn't be addictions. Getting past this roadblock is going to be the toughest job you have in facing your reality, and it is very difficult to do this on your own. But that's exactly why it's so important that you do so.

2. **The past.** I'm going to tell you something right now

that you might not realize: there isn't a single adult walking around on this planet who doesn't have something he or she regrets about the past. If you have lots of regrets, you are so completely not alone. Life is a complicated journey, and no one gets through that journey without a few things they wish hadn't happened. Still, even if you understand this, it's easy to convince yourself that the regretful or embarrassing or damaging stuff in your past is worse than most other people's and is impossible to overcome. I'm here to tell you that this isn't true. Your past may be filled with things you wish you could make disappear, but the only way to move forward is to face those things, accept the effect they had on your life, and then acknowledge that your past doesn't need to define you forever.

3. **Your failures.** People fail. I've failed more times than I can count. Everyone I know and love has failed, in one way or another, on numerous occasions, and I'm sure I don't know about *all* of their failures. If you're alive, you're going to fail many, many times. I understand how hard it is to come back from some failures. In the moment, they all seem awful, and sometimes it is truly difficult to recover from the damage that was done. Sometimes failure is so hard to accept that you just try to pretend it never happened. That's a problem, though, because ignoring your failures makes it easier to repeat them. What you need to do instead is allow those failures and the lessons you learned from them to guide you toward your goals. But you can only do that if you face them head-on.

4. **Opinions.** "I don't care what anybody thinks!" How many times have you said that in your life? Has it ever actually been true? If you're like most people, not only do you care about what other people think, but their opinions have had a huge effect on you. Maybe your mother made you feel like a disappointment. Maybe a teacher told you you'd never get ahead. Maybe a coach told you that being a starter wasn't in your future. Or maybe it wasn't anything that black-and-white. Instead, you just have the sense that people think you're only okay or not terribly smart or not particularly talented or kind of a bore. These opinions can create a huge roadblock for you, because you can begin to see yourself as you think other people see you. And this has gotten so much worse since social media came around. Now, I'm not going to suggest that you ignore what other people think, because that would be like me telling you not to breathe. But an important part of facing your reality is acknowledging others' opinions, putting them in their proper context (who's saying these things, and do they have an agenda?), and then deciding how much truth there is in any of these opinions.

Roadblocks are tough to get past, or they wouldn't be roadblocks. If you could just drive right over them, they wouldn't be blocking you at all. But unlike that roadblock that kept you off the highway the other day, you *can* get around these roadblocks. The first thing you have to do is acknowledge that the roadblock is there—face your reality—and then you can figure out how to get around it. I'm going to let a fellow Rehabber speak here to help us work on this.

Carly had lots of help in avoiding her reality. For twelve years, her family and her friends constantly told her that her man was the best thing that had ever happened to her. If she would complain about something abusive that he did, they'd take his side and then pile on by telling Carly that her issues were all in her head. She was with a great man who treated her right, they claimed; she was just going to have to get over herself.

And for a dozen years, Carly was convinced that this was the case. Deep inside, she knew something was terribly wrong with her life, that she was getting so much less than she deserved, and that the way she was being treated was slowly eating away at her. But it was so much easier to run away from this truth. Things weren't *that* bad, right?

But one night, the situation got more physical and more dangerous, and Carly's young daughter—who'd had to witness all of the past abuse—asked her how much more she was going to take. Carly realized that she didn't have a good answer for her child, and she couldn't continue to put the two of them at risk any longer. So, she packed up what she could, took a twenty-dollar debit card and twenty dollars in cash, and left with her daughter for a shelter. There, she met with a domestic violence therapist who finally helped her see that she'd been a victim of abuse for more than a decade. Carly had convinced herself that she was worthless and somehow deserving of the emotional, verbal, and sometimes physical mistreatment she had received. But now that she was facing the reality of her situation head-on, she knew she could never go back to deluding herself again.

"It was difficult at first to face the truths," she told me, "because I didn't want to see what they really were about. I also knew that if I was going to live what is left of my life in peace, I was going to have to face them and either forgive or stay angry all the time."

Leaving was the break that Carly needed to see the world as it really was, to understand what had been done to her and how she'd been forcing herself to live in delusion for so long. She started going regularly to therapy, which truly opened her eyes.

"It took me leaving to finally realize that I had always put myself last and took care of everyone else's needs, and that I am worth much more than what he said I was. I started seeing things for what they really were and started seeing the things that should have been a warning sign for me. I had sacrificed so much that it was hard to ask for help, but once I started asking for help I found myself in the process."

The hard work that Carly has committed herself to has already paid off for her in a big way. Her relationships with her family, which had suffered considerable damage as the abuse she was suffering went on, are now getting back on track. She's even managed to forgive the man who was so responsible for her misery.

"For the first time in my life, I'm in a much happier place. I've cut the negative people out of my life and I'm focusing on the positive. I've had a rough life. But now I feel better about myself and know that any issues that come along I will handle with my head held high and confidence in my stride."

Carly was facing a huge roadblock in her life because of her friends' and family's opinion that she was the luckiest woman in the world to be with the man who was abusing her. And she convinced herself for a long time that their opinion was right. But when she faced the reality that their opinion was deeply wrong, she was able to get past that roadblock, to discover that she'd been surviving in an unacceptable situation, and to move on to a much, much better place.

It's Time for Brutal Honesty

All of us need to move forward in our lives. If you aren't moving forward—if you aren't doing more to reach your goals, setting new ones for yourself, and trying your best to live in fulfillment of your purpose (which we'll talk about a lot in the next chapter)—then I'll be honest with you: you're dying. If you stay stuck in the same bad situation indefinitely, then you're letting your life waste away. On the other hand, if you take even a tiny step forward every day—even if you have to crawl—you're making progress toward becoming the best version of yourself, to being the greatest you. There's only one way you can take these steps, though: you have to be real with yourself.

Let's work on this together. I want you to take some time right now to make an honest assessment of where you are in your life. For example, where do you stand with your family? With your other relationships? With your physical condition? With your job? How does where you are right now match up with where you want to be?

I've always heard that the one person you should never lie to is your anesthesiologist. If you're about to go into surgery and you tell the guy putting you under that you haven't had a drink in a year even though you took six shots the night before, the anesthesiologist can give you the wrong dosage and do some serious damage. Well, I would say there's one other person you should never lie to, and that's yourself. The reason is pretty much the same. If you're trying to make moves to get your life going in the right direction and you lie to yourself about your situation, you're likely to make the wrong moves that could affect you in the worst possible ways. The key to your success is being brutally honest with yourself.

I understand why you might not want to be super-honest with yourself. Sometimes some of the hardest truths to face are those that get to the very essence of how we define ourselves as human beings. Maybe you've spent the last fifteen years defining yourself as a wife, but the brutally honest truth is that your marriage has been lifeless for a long time. You can barely stand being in the same room with your spouse, and you haven't said a truly loving thing to each other in years. Your marriage is hollow, but you've so completely defined yourself by your marriage that you have no idea who you would be if you were honest enough to admit that it is in shambles.

Or maybe you finally see that the reason you hate getting out of bed in the morning is that you despise what your job has become—but when people ask you about yourself, the first thing you tell them about is your work. You know deep inside that you have to get out of that job before it kills you, but what are you going to say to people when they ask you about yourself in the future? Hey, you know what happened to me and football. When the Colts cut me, I was so deflated that I couldn't even leave my parents' house.

Often, we know something is over, but we can't deal with what it means for it to be over. It has become such a part of who we are that we're not sure who we would be without it, even though it's causing us harm. That's tough, I know. As I mentioned at the beginning of this chapter, I lied to myself about the fact that my football playing career was over for a long time before I finally faced it. I convinced myself I had to do anything necessary to keep playing football, because "football player" was the only thing I really thought I was as a person. I had to discover who I was underneath the NFL player, because that was the only way I could have a meaningful life going forward.

There's a good chance that you're reading these pages and saying to yourself, "You don't get it, Trent. You don't understand what I'm going through. You don't understand my struggle. You want me to be honest with myself and take steps to move forward, but you don't know my situation, because in *my* situation moving forward is a lot easier said than done."

Let's make a deal right now: I'll do everything I can to help you, but you've got to give up that easier-said-than-done mind-set. It's just a tool for allowing yourself to stay stuck, an excuse for why you can't make things better. That's fine if you want to live the rest of your life unhappy, in which case I'm not sure why you're reading this book. But "easier said than done" is at the very best like taking an aspirin when you've dislocated your shoulder. It might be a tiny bit helpful briefly, but the pain is still going to be there and the cause of the pain isn't going to get better until you give it some serious attention.

Yes, I get it. Facing your reality is hard, especially if it means losing your current identity. But what most people in this situation fail to understand is that while they might lose who they *think* they are by facing their reality, they'll wind up finding out who they *truly* are instead. There's a very good chance that the thing you're hanging on to isn't who you were meant to be at all.

This is probably a good time to tell you about how I became involved with motivational speaking.

Are You Scared?

Let me say this right at the top: the first time someone suggested that I speak in front of an audience, I thought he was mistaking me for someone else. Speaking was my biggest fear. I realize I'm not alone; many studies show that people fear public speaking more than they fear dying. As they say, people would rather be in the casket than giving the eulogy. At the same time, I had to do something to move forward in my life. I knew football was over, but I was hanging on to it out of fear and the belief that if I lost football I would lose my life. Would people still love me? Would they still support me? Would they still talk about me? Would I even really *exist*?

A guy I knew from Baylor named Jonathan Evans invited me to do my first major speaking engagement. My first thought was, *He's tripping. I'm a football player. I'm not a speaker.* But he told me that he was sure that I had something inside of me that I didn't even know about, something that he could see about me that I couldn't see about myself. "I'm gonna give you an opportunity to speak at my church," he said.

I was so afraid that I immediately came up with three

questions I was sure would end this entirely unexpected conversation. I was doing what so many of us do when faced with an opportunity to change our lives: we give ourselves reasons not to be great. We live in our limitations. We think about all the reasons why we can't do something.

"Who am I speaking to?" I asked.

"A bunch of teenagers."

My eyes flew open. "I'm out of it. There's no way I'm doing my first speaking engagement in front of a bunch of teenagers." I remembered what I was like as a teenager, and I imagined standing in front of a group of people who were like I was back then—looking bored and as if they'd rather be anywhere else on earth.

Jonathan challenged me. "Are you scared, Trent?"

"No, I'm not scared," I said defensively, though I was at least *a little* scared. "All right, let me ask you another question: How many am I speaking to?"

"Five thousand."

"Five thousand for my first speaking engagement? No, I'm not doing it."

Jonathan got this little smile on his face. "Are you sure you're not scared? I'm telling you, I see something in you that you don't even see in yourself. You gotta do this."

I wasn't about to admit how terrifying this was all starting to sound to me. I began to process the information I had. *Okay, five thousand teenagers. I can talk football; that won't bore them too much. I'll go onstage for a minute and then get off.*

"Okay, one more question: How long am I speaking for?"

"You're speaking for five minutes."

He may as well have said five hours. "Bro, that is way

too long. What am I gonna say? I can give you two minutes; that's it."

"Five minutes. Do it, Trent. You'll be great at it."

This entire conversation had thrown me off, but I had to acknowledge that people had been suggesting similar things to me for a long time. Even when I was a kid, people told me that they saw me in front of big crowds, inspiring others. I thought they were talking about me catching touchdown passes in big games. But maybe there was something more to my life.

As you already know, that speaking engagement went great. Even though it was one of the most fearful, confidence-shaking things I've done, it turned out to be the most impactful for my life. I don't think I've ever had an audience so locked in—the kids weren't even blinking. Afterward, they asked me all kinds of questions about life, about dreams, about purpose. They saw me as someone who could help them get the most out of their lives. I was shocked by their response. Now, this didn't get me all the way to where I had to go; I still had to come face-to-face with the situations I told you about at the beginning of this chapter. But I was starting to get it. I was starting to accept that my current situation didn't have to be my final destination. My current reality didn't have to be my final one.

Right around this time, I went back to a Bible my mother had given me. On the cover was an NFL football, though the NFL in this case actually stood for "new found life." On the first page of this Bible, my mother had quoted Jeremiah 29:11: "'For I know the plans I have for you,' declares the LORD, 'plans to prosper you and not to harm you, plans to give you hope and a future.'" The funny thing was, I never picked up that Bible when I was trying to make it in the NFL.

But now it all made sense to me. My "new found life" was not football; it was RehabTime and helping people. To this day, that scripture fuels my faith more than anything.

Taking the First Steps to Winning Your War

At this moment, I want you to make a real decision to stop running from your battles. You have to understand that you're one choice away from a new beginning and one commitment away from a new life. This moment can be the first step to changing your life forever. Don't let the "How am I going to win this battle?" question keep you from facing that battle. The *how* isn't as important as the *why*. I'm living proof that the how will reveal itself during the journey. You simply have to start the journey. Go back and look at the stories in this chapter. Look at my story, or Carly's. Do you see yourself in either of these stories? Even if you don't, there's a lot to be learned from witnessing what happened to us when we accepted our realities and began to move forward with our lives.

So, here's how we're going to do this. I'm going to end this chapter with a few questions that will help you focus on the task of facing your reality. Take the time to answer them—being super-real with yourself—before going further into the book:

- Where are you in your life today?
- What excuses have you been making for your situation that you can throw away right now?

- What are you hanging on to because of fear?
- What is the biggest lie you're telling yourself?
- What kind of truth do you see once you get rid of the lies?

Once you've answered these questions, you've taken a big step toward moving your life forward. You're on your way, and I'm proud of you. Let's keep it going now by taking a serious look at your purpose.

2

WHAT'S YOUR PURPOSE?

As you already know, I was convinced from the time I was very young that I was meant to be a great football player. Nothing else mattered; I was certain that football was the way I was going to make my mark on the world. If anyone had ever suggested that I would wind up on a different path, I would have ignored them. And if anyone had ever told me I would end up reaching millions through speaking engagements and inspirational videos—that doing so was my purpose—I would have thought that they were smoking something.

I was completely missing the truth. In reality, the signs of my true purpose were there from the time I was a little kid. When I was young, I used to go to evangelical conferences with my mother a lot. I was the third of three brothers, and my mom liked having me along with her on these trips that she was taking for her church. I particularly remember one seminar in New Orleans that I went to with her when I was five. Even though I was really young, I connected hard with the speakers. At one point, the evangelist asked us all to stand up, and when I did, I felt a gust of wind that I just knew was the Holy Spirit—and it was so strong that it knocked me down. This really made an impression on me, and afterward I talked to my mother about it.

"Did you feel that?" I said.

"Feel what?"

"That gust of wind. I just feel the power of God over me."

She admitted that she didn't feel the same, and then looked at me and smiled. "That's because you're being called to do something great, Trent."

That was the first time anyone said something like that to me, and when I heard it, it just felt right. Even at five, I felt that God had put me here to do something great.

When I started playing football not long after that, I assumed it was the great thing I was supposed to do. I was really good at it, and football stars were famous, with lots of people looking up to them. It made perfect sense, even more so when I starred in high school and college. But of course, I was wrong about that. At the time, Mom saw things the same way I did, but now we both realize that football was just preparing me for who I was supposed to become. At the time, though, I wasn't correctly reading the messages I was getting.

And people *did* try to get messages to me. I remember going to church with my quarterback when I was playing arena football in Tulsa. We didn't want anyone to notice us, so we sat in the back of the church and did our best not to be seen. It didn't work out. The pastor started ministering to the congregation, and at one point, he looked over where we were sitting and made eye contact with both of us.

"Why don't the two of you come down to the front?" he said.

I looked behind me to see if maybe he was talking to someone else, but there was no one there. No, he wanted *us* in the front of the church. Sheepishly, we got up and moved forward. I was wearing a RehabTime T-shirt because I'd just recently started the program, but the program was still pretty small. There was no way the pastor could have known what RehabTime was or what I was doing then with my spare time.

As soon as we sat down in the front, the pastor came up close to me and said, "There's something special about you." I thought maybe he recognized me from the team. But then he asked me what I did, and when I told him that I played football, he took that in for a second and then said, "No, that's not it. I see you speaking. I see you traveling the world and touching souls and reaching people with your message."

That seemed completely crazy to me. This was before my first big speaking engagement, and as I told you in the last chapter, I was not at all comfortable with speaking in front of people. How could that possibly be what I was supposed to do with my life? Sure, I was making videos every now and then, but there was no way *public* speaking was my purpose. I was going back to the NFL; *that* was my purpose.

Respectfully, I let the pastor know that I thought he might be mistaken. But he waved away my skepticism. "I see you reaching millions of people across the world," he continued. "I see you speaking on stages all over the planet." Then he locked eyes with me and said, "It's coming for you very soon. Just know that it is and start preparing your life."

He seemed awfully convinced, but I still wasn't going along with it. I was a football player, and I wasn't going to change my plans because someone, even a man of the cloth, thought he saw something different in me, something that made no sense to me with regard to who I was as a person.

Not long after this, I was on Trinity Broadcasting Network for a piece evangelist Dwight Thompson was doing with a few NFL players about how they were finding purpose in their lives. We were mostly talking about football, with a couple of mentions about what I'd started doing with RehabTime, which, again, still wasn't much of anything at that point.

Toward the end of the interview, Thompson said something to me that seemed to come from nowhere. "You're going to be one of the greatest soul winners of this generation," he said. "You're gonna help a lot of people."

So people were seeing this in me. But every time I heard it, I was certain they were wrong. My vision was football, and I thought my whole life was about that. Everything else in life was for other people—for them and for their purposes in life. My father was a pastor, and he was awesome, inspiring lots of people. But that was him, not me. My Sundays were going to be about a different gig.

But it wasn't long after that TBN interview that I started to realize that God didn't intend football to be my life. While I was seeing the game as my everything, he was using it to prepare me for my true purpose. Through football, he let me get a taste of notoriety and money and fame, helping me understand that for me those things were empty. And because of that, I was much better prepared to handle all of those things when they came along in the life I was meant to lead.

You Are Purpose

Before we really get into this, I want to make an important point that I think a lot of people misunderstand. Purpose is not something tied to a job or a title or a platform. It isn't something you search for or take a bunch of tests to discover. You *are* purpose. You were created for purpose *on* purpose, and your life is purpose. Purpose is your true self. It's something you discover inside, and you can get there only by owning everything about you.

Now, when I talk about how at first I mistook football for my purpose and then realized that my real purpose was something else, I'm not saying that RehabTime specifically is my purpose. It's not. RehabTime is simply an avenue for my purpose, for me to be who I am, for my life to be used in the best possible way. Speaking and making videos are the tools I use to do what I was put here to do, but those tools are not my purpose. There's an important difference here. My purpose is to help people and to inspire people. That's who I am— that's who I was when I was that little boy traveling with my mother, and it's who I've always been. And that's what I was put here to do. Because I own that, I can make a contribution with it. RehabTime just happens to be how I'm making that contribution right now.

When you understand that your life *is* purpose, you realize you can use your life in any number of ways to make this world a better place, even if it's just by giving someone a compliment. Because that's what purpose is: it's using your life for the betterment of the world. So, yeah, I found my purpose in speaking and in creating RehabTime, not because RehabTime is my purpose but because it helped me find myself and my avenue of reaching out. Once I found out who I really was, the tools fell into place.

I'm going to keep coming back to this point, but let me hit it hard right now: everything about you—including your flaws, your imperfections, and your past—exists to be used to improve the world. It may not always feel that way to you, but I know this for a fact. None of us are here just to take up space.

And here's the other thing: sometimes the avenue doesn't open up right away. Maybe you've had the experience where you think you understand who you are and what you were put here to do, but all the avenues to doing it seem closed off. If you stay true to yourself, if you keep owning who you are, and you keep moving forward with the understanding that your life exists to be used to bring good to the world, that'll change. That's what happened with Christine.

When Christine was eight, her mother, who was a nurse at an outpatient psychiatry office, brought home a personality test. This test showed Christine that she was especially interested in helping others find their true selves. She began to tell everyone that she was going to be a psychiatrist when she grew up, and she was convinced that this was what she was put on earth to do.

But things didn't turn out exactly the way she expected.

When she was eighteen, she gave birth to her first child, meaning, for her, that college was off the table. Instead, she went to trade school and took a job as an office assistant.

"I was young and confused, and now I had this baby that depended on me," she told me. "My dream was crushed, but little did I know my calling was still very much alive. Five years into my career as an office assistant, I found a position in a psychiatry office. It was still not my dream, but I figured I may as well assist another person in fulfilling their dreams, because it was too late for me. It was during my time at this office that my calling found me."

Christine found herself getting into deep conversations with the clients scheduled to see the psychiatrist. "I loved each and every one of them without judgment. Somehow, I understood them.

"I started to receive letters from clients who stated they were on the verge of taking their own life until words I spoke to them changed their perspective. I remember one particular young man who said to me, 'Even if my depression never goes away, you said things to me that will change how I think about it forever.' That day, that moment, that young man was God confirming to me my calling here on earth. It was this moment that I looked at the Bible verse Romans 12:8—'If [your gift is] to encourage, then give encouragement'—in a whole new light. It just clicked. This was why I was created."

Christine knew this was something more than just a very good day at work because, she said, she was experiencing "unexplainable divine joy that taps into our strongest strength and deepest love." Soon after this, she got to work becoming a certified life coach and speaker.

"This is a gift given to me by God. I was placed here to encourage those who need uplifting. The best way I can describe the difference between a job and a calling is you can retire from a job, but you cannot retire from a calling."

Christine makes a great point here, one that goes back to what I was saying about you *being* purpose. When purpose is who you are, when purpose is what you were created for, when purpose is your life, then that purpose is with you every single day—and if it's not, something isn't right.

Living Your Purpose

There's no way you're going to be the greatest you if you aren't living your actual purpose. I can tell you from personal experience: I didn't come close to being who I was supposed to be or the kind of person I wanted to be until I stopped believing my purpose was football and accepted that my real role in this world was to inspire and help people. And as you already know, when I was pursuing my false purpose, I was filled with frustration, unhappiness, and anxiety. And if you aren't living your purpose, there's a good chance that you're feeling many of those same things right now. We're going to work on that, because living your purpose is going to make so much more in your life fall into place.

When I talk to people about purpose, one of the most common things I hear is, "I don't know what my purpose is" or, "I don't think I have a purpose." To get to the second part first, let me just say that every person on this planet has a purpose of some kind. We were all put here for a reason. God didn't create you just so you could wander around for a while and then die. There's a reason you're here, and that reason is important not only to you but to the other people you touch, because every person's purpose involves touching the lives of others in some way. Your purpose is always something that's bigger than you. We are meant to contribute to the world, not just spend some time in it.

So, let's get that "I don't have a purpose" thing out of the way right now. You do have a purpose, and it's a powerful thing that goes way beyond your own life. So the question is, what is your purpose? If you don't know, it's very possible that you don't really know what purpose is about, so let's deal with that.

Before I talk about what purpose is, I want to talk some more about what it isn't. Purpose isn't about success. Not specifically, anyway. I think this might be the single biggest mistake people make when they think about their purpose. They think it has to make them a lot of money. Or that it has to make them famous. Or that they have to be the boss or something. But purpose isn't any of those things. Sure, it might lead to one or more of those things, but that's just a by-product. And in my experience, your purpose never comes out of plans for success. If you say, "I want to be a rapper because then I'll be a big star," there's a good chance that following that path isn't going to lead you to your purpose. If you say, "I want to be a rapper because I feel like I have something to say that is going to deliver a valuable message to a lot of people," that's something else entirely. Then you might really be talking about your purpose. But not if the first thing that comes to mind is making it big.

In the same way, you may feel that something that really matters to you can't be your purpose because you can't see how you could make a living at it or get a nice house with it or get lots of acclaim for it. You need to think that over. I know far more happy people who are living modestly while fulfilling their purpose than I do happy people who are making a lot of money but doing something they hate or that makes them feel like a fraud every day. And your purpose doesn't even have to be your job. It might not be tied up in money or status at all. Maybe your purpose is volunteering to help people learn how to read. Maybe it's coaching a neighborhood kids' basketball team. Maybe it's donating a chunk of your time to church or a local school or to a community center. You're not going to get rich or famous doing any of those things, but that could be exactly what you were put here to do.

Let's get back to that key point again: purpose is who you are. It is why you were created. It is how you are contributing to the world. When you are living your purpose, you feel as though you're making a difference. It doesn't have to be a huge difference, like curing a disease or talking someone out of killing himself. It could be anything that makes people's lives better even in a tiny way. Maybe you're a bus driver, and the way you greet your passengers at the start of the day makes them feel a little bit better about going to work. That's a great thing. That's having a genuine impact on lives. If that feels right to you, don't run away from it because there aren't any bus drivers with five million followers on Instagram. And definitely don't listen to that voice in your head that says that because you're a bus driver, you don't have any purpose other than getting people from one destination to another.

Think about it this way: the right words said at the right time can make a gigantic difference. You can, for example, change someone's life with a Facebook post. That's what happened with me. I started posting videos and sending out messages of inspiration, which led to positive changes in people's lives. And once that started happening, I realized that the things people had been saying to me since I was five were right and that by doing this inspirational work, I was living my purpose.

So, if you feel that you don't know what your purpose is, answer this question for me: What are you doing that makes a difference in the lives of others? Again, don't get caught up in how much of a difference or how many others. Just give that some thought. What are you doing that has the most positive effect? And how do you feel when you're doing it? There's a very good chance that when you're doing these things, those are the moments when you feel most "right." If that's the case, then you're probably much closer to your purpose than you ever realized.

Running Away from Your Purpose

In the last chapter, I pushed you to be completely real with yourself. I'm going to be doing that a lot in this book, and I'm doing it again right now. It's an important part of our work together, so I really need you to commit to this. Here's your next opportunity to face the truth. Yes, it's possible that if you don't know what your purpose is, it's because you just haven't discovered that thing yet. But something else might be going on here: you might not know what your purpose is because you don't want to see it or you don't want *that thing* to be your purpose.

I know all about this one. As I said before, long before I ever made a video or got up on a stage, people had been telling me that they saw me speaking to and inspiring people. If I had been completely real with myself, I would have accepted that I was going to contribute much more to the world doing this than I would ever contribute playing football. After all, besides providing a temporary thrill to fans after I made a big gain or scored a touchdown, football was really all about me. Speaking and offering inspiration, however, was a way I could go outside of myself and touch other lives.

But here's the thing: I really didn't want my purpose to be speaking. From my perspective, speaking wasn't something you aspired to. It wasn't a sexy platform, the way football was. I always knew that speakers could help people if they spoke the truth, but it just wasn't anything I could get excited about. When I was growing up, my friends and I didn't sit around saying things like, "Hey, you know what I'm gonna be when I grow up? I'm gonna be a *speaker*." I had a vision for myself, and being a speaker wasn't part of that vision in any way.

I'm sure in some part of my mind I knew that my real purpose was right there waiting to be discovered, but I kept looking away from it and toward football because football better fit how I saw myself and the life I thought I wanted to lead.

This kind of thing comes up all the time when I'm talking to people about purpose. They'll say things to me like, "Well, yeah, I'm really good at being a salesclerk, but what kind of purpose is that?" Maybe this person has dreams of becoming a TV personality or a CEO, so she can't see that what she's good at is something that makes a real contribution and can affect the lives of others in a positive way.

You see, there's a big difference between purpose and dreams. Dreams are usually influenced by the world. The world celebrates certain professions and accomplishments, so we tend to dream about being the kind of person who attains those things. I'm not saying that you shouldn't have dreams. Dreaming of a bigger life for yourself can be motivational and push you to do more than you would do otherwise, and it's entirely possible that you have it within yourself to fulfill these dreams. But you need to take stock of your dreams and think about whether they're achievable or just fantasies. If you dream of curing a disease, but you don't like science, there's a pretty good chance you're never going to fulfill that dream. If you dream of being the next Beyoncé but you're too shy to sing in front of a crowd, you might want to limit that dream to when you're in the shower and take a closer look at what you were really meant to do.

I've found that an awful lot of people fail to see their purpose because that purpose doesn't put them in the spotlight. But let me make something clear to you right now: purpose is *never* about the spotlight. Sometimes your purpose will get you to the spotlight, but that's just a by-product. If you're living your purpose, you're doing the thing you were put on this earth to do. If that leads to your becoming a household name or making big bucks or winning awards, great, but if those things are going to happen, it'll be because you're living your purpose. It doesn't work the other way around.

So instead of rejecting what may very well be your true purpose because it doesn't match your dreams or it doesn't give you a big enough platform, think about what you were really meant to do. There is something honorable about nearly every pursuit as long as you follow that pursuit with passion and dedication. And the world needs people who are living their purpose in every area. Being a dedicated salesclerk makes a meaningful contribution—just think about the last time you needed help in a store and someone pointed you in the right direction. How good did that make you feel? Yeah, a salesclerk isn't going to walk the red carpet for being a salesclerk, but the sooner you realize that purpose isn't about walking the red carpet, the sooner you'll stop ignoring your purpose and start living a more fulfilled life.

Finding Your Purpose—Without Looking

So, if you're ready to stop running away from your purpose, how do you actually find out what your purpose is? For many of you, the simple act of no longer denying what you've been denying for years might be enough to reveal your purpose to you. For the rest of you, I have some simple advice: stop looking for it. I know that sounds crazy, especially since I've spent this entire chapter telling you how important finding your purpose is, but this might be a necessary step for you. Have you ever had the experience of trying really hard to remember something? It's right there, but the harder you try, the further away it seems to get. You finally stop trying, and a few hours later the thing you were trying to remember just pops into your head. It's possible that, for you, finding your purpose is going to be something like that. If you tell yourself that you're not going to get up from that chair until you know what your purpose is, there's a really good chance that you're going to be sitting in that chair for a long time. Stop fixating on this and try a few exercises instead.

Your purpose is something you discover when you peel back the layers of your life and see who you truly are. Since that's the case, try to rediscover who you are as a person. If you're like most people I know, you're in reaction mode most of the time. You're reacting to the needs of your family or the needs of your job or the needs of your friends. Maybe you're reacting to input from social media or from a show you're watching on television. When you're in reaction mode, you're not really fully present as yourself. You're doing what you need to do to get through a situation, and that means putting the full application of your personality and your values on hold. Unless your purpose is purely about reacting—and it isn't going to be for most of us—then you're never going to see yourself for who you really are when you're in reaction mode. So, pull back. Give yourself some time to think about who you are when the world isn't pulling at you. What do you *really* care about? What *really* makes you happy? What are your *real* goals? When do you feel most satisfied with how your life is going? When do you feel you're making some kind of difference? When you start to think about these things and answer these questions, you see yourself at your most genuine. And once you see that person, you'll begin to see what you were created to be.

Another thing to do is to think about your pain. I realize

that thinking about the stuff that has hurt you the most isn't a fun exercise, but it's an important one, so let's play this out. Remember that your purpose comes in your service to others. Well, if you hadn't gone through the things you've gone through, you wouldn't be qualified to help others when they go through something similar. That's certainly how it was for me. I know what it's like to feel that you've lost your everything. I also know what it's like to overcome that, so I can confidently tell others that they can overcome what they're going through. Those are the kinds of people you want in your life, and that's the kind of person you'll be if you're living your purpose.

A lot of people try to give you a map without hiking the trail. They'll give you advice for fixing a problem, but they've never experienced the problem themselves. Your purpose comes out of the trails you've actually hiked and the problems you've encountered. That's when you can really help others. When I offer advice, sometimes people say to me, "Trent, that's easy for you to say." And I say, "Yes, it is—because I've been through what you're going through. I've been through the struggle, so I can talk to you with confidence." So, explore your pain. Explore the struggles you've overcome. Even if you're struggling hard now, I'm sure you can remember a time when you got past a big roadblock. Your experience with that might point you toward your purpose.

Another tool is trial and error. Put things out into the world and see what happens. Think about all of the different ways you interact with the world. What would happen if you played with your approach to these things? What if you put a little more of yourself out there on social media? What if you shared an idea with your boss or offered to do something new at work? What if you shared something you knew a lot about with people who could benefit from your expertise? This sort of thing might be way outside of your comfort zone, but often we benefit the most when we get beyond that zone, and doing so here might lead to some big discoveries. You might get a great reaction from other people in your life. You might expose a strength you didn't realize you had or discover that something you never appreciated about yourself has real value to others. In all likelihood, a bunch of this stuff is going to lead nowhere, but if you make a conscious effort to put more things out into the world, there's a good chance that one of them is going to stick—and your purpose might very well reveal itself to you through this exercise.

Now, let's get back to one of the key points: our purpose in life is to be used. I don't mean that in a foul or abusive or disruptive way, but I do believe our purpose in life is to be used in a powerful and impactful way. When you realize that your life exists to be used—for whatever reason—you start to understand why God put you here in the first place. So, let's do one more exercise. How can people use you—without making you feel like you're being taken advantage of—in a way that allows your talents, your wisdom, and your life experience to benefit them? If you could make just one piece of yourself available to anyone who wanted to use it, what would that piece be? There may be a big clue to your purpose in the answer to that question.

Now look at the results of these exercises. What did you learn when you took some time to get out of reaction mode? What did you discover about your pain? What happened when you put some new things out there? What's the part of you that others can use the most?

Now ask yourself the question again: What's my purpose? There's a good chance that you're going to have an answer now that you didn't have before.

Knowing When You've Found It

Okay, so you've asked yourself the question and an answer has come to you. How do you know you have the real answer? This is maybe the most common question people have when I talk about finding purpose. How do you know when you've actually found it?

One of the clearest indications is a feeling of peace that wasn't there before. That's certainly what happened with me. As you know, when I was running from my real purpose and trying to make football fill that role, I was constantly stressed out, and I experienced a strong sense of discomfort every single day. I thought this was because I wasn't getting my break in the NFL or because arena football wasn't creating an opportunity for me to play on Sundays, but I understand now that it was because I wasn't doing what God intended for me to do. Once I really started building RehabTime and started to do more videos and go on more stages to speak to groups of people, I discovered a peace that had eluded me my entire adult life. These new activities weren't a struggle. Instead, they were giving me a deep satisfaction that I didn't know was possible. That's when I knew I was living my purpose.

You'll also get some big clues you're on the right track

from the way people respond to you. As you go through the exercises we talked about in the last section, take a look at how people react to what you're doing. Has something changed? Are the people around you treating you a little bit differently—better, hopefully—than they were before? Are new people coming into your life who are seeing you in ways that others haven't in the past? This isn't accidental. When you're living your purpose, you're making a meaningful contribution to the world. And even if that contribution is a relatively small thing, people react differently when they feel that someone is contributing something of substance to the world. Are you seeing any of this in your own life?

The other way you can know you've found your purpose is by asking, "Can I see myself continuing to do this?" Purpose is not something you do every now and then. Remember what Christine said about never retiring from a calling. It isn't like being nicer to people at Christmastime or making a New Year's resolution. Those things tend to fade pretty quickly as a little time passes. Sure, people's purposes take on new forms and go in new directions over the years, but those are the avenues, not purpose itself. Purpose isn't a short-term thing. It's the thing that defines you more than anything else. You are purpose. So, if you think you've found something that might be your purpose, how are you going to feel about living that purpose every day for the rest of your life? If you're good with that, then you might very well be living your purpose. If you're thinking, *Well, I could do this for a little while, but then I'm gonna want to do something else*, you probably haven't found it yet.

Look at it another way: Is this the thing that's going to get you up in the morning? I always tell people that I used to love to sleep, but then my reality became better than my dreams. I want that to be true for you too. If you wake up in the morning ready and excited about doing something that you're doing all the time, then you've probably found your purpose. When you're living your purpose, you sleep to recharge, not to escape your reality.

That's how you'll know. If you're excited about seeing a new day, if people are reacting positively to your contribution, and if you feel a strong sense of peace about what you're doing, you've found your purpose. Congratulations. If you've gotten to this stage, you're a long way toward becoming the best version of yourself, the greatest you. And if you're not there yet, we'll keep working away at it. Maybe circle back to this chapter after you've read a few more, as those chapters might give you some new tools to help you here.

Some Purposeful Steps

Regardless of where you are at this point, take a little time to answer these questions—being completely real, of course—before you go on to the next chapter.

- Do you believe you have a purpose?
- Are you more concerned with how big your platform is than with what you're contributing to the world?
- Can you tell the difference between purpose and dreams?
- What are you already doing that is making life better for the people around you?
- What gets you out of bed in the morning?

Take some time to really think about these questions. You're doing a lot of important work here, so take a minute to acknowledge what you've already accomplished. I'm impressed with your willingness to dive deep into this material. Now we're going to move on to something that stops a lot of people cold when they think about making more out of their lives, and you'll see how it never needs to stop you again.

3

EVEN IF YOU'VE HAD
SOME BAD CHAPTERS,
YOUR STORY CAN
STILL END WELL

We all love stories, whether we're reading a book or going to a movie or watching TV. So, here's a story for you:

A baby is born, and from the moment that baby takes her first breath, everybody loves that baby and gives her everything she wants and needs. As the baby gets older, she makes lots of friends, does great in school, becomes a star athlete, and develops an amazing singing voice. She picks a career, gets a big promotion right away, falls in love, has a couple of terrific kids who turn out as wonderfully as she turned out, and she lives a long life where she gets to do everything she ever wanted to do.

There are two things about that story, right? First, it's boring. Who wants to hear a story where everything works out perfectly all the time? Second, it's completely unrealistic. If you saw that story on Netflix, you'd click it off in about five minutes, because the person who made that show has no idea how life actually works.

Now think about the stories you love. They probably have some big complications in them, don't they? Sometimes those complications come right at the start of the story: The hero gets in serious trouble, and it's going to take a miracle to get him out of it. Or maybe things are going along fine, and then he gets slammed with something that turns his whole life upside down, and he spends the rest of the story dealing with that. That's a way more interesting story, isn't it? It's also way more realistic, because everybody's story has some bad chapters in it. But a few bad chapters don't mean that the story is guaranteed to be a tragedy. Even with a few (or a lot of) bad chapters, your story can still turn out great.

One of the biggest reasons people don't make positive changes in their lives is that they're chained to the past. They feel that what they've already been through means they have to go through the same kinds of negative things over and over. If you've had bad relationships before, you're destined to keep having bad relationships. If you failed at a job, you're going to fail at all of your jobs. If you've gotten caught up in addictions or dangerous habits, you're going to stay addicted forever. A big percentage of the people I talk to are completely convinced they are defined by their past and that they can't do anything about it. Maybe you're one of these people. I get it. Why would you take a step toward change if every step you took in the past has been filled with pain? It was hard for me to believe in new beginnings when pain, failure, and setbacks were all that I ever knew.

Or maybe you think that you *might* be able to make something more out of your life, but the world isn't going to let you do that, and your peers aren't going to let you, either. And that makes you crazy, because these are the same people who are telling you that you've got to get your stuff together and make some big improvements. But as soon as you start to work on it, they start telling you about the imperfections in your plan or how you're not fixing yourself the right way. You've gotta get those people out of your head. We're going to talk a lot more about that in the next chapter. But for now, let me just say that I know how hard it is to hear that kind of stuff. Most of us live in fear of being judged by others. In fact, the number one fear in the world is thought to be public speaking, and the reason is that people are afraid of standing in front of other people and being judged by them. And when people judge you, it never seems that they're judging you in a positive way. No, they're seeking out your imperfections, your flaws, either to bring you down or in an effort to "fix" you.

Fear of being judged keeps a lot of us from doing anything significant to make our lives better. Improving your life is tough work, and what's the point of going through all of that work if people are just going to judge you anyway?

But here's the thing: they're going to judge you no matter what you do. If you do nothing, they'll judge you for that. If you make a huge effort to improve your life, they'll judge you for that too. And they'll judge you for everything in between. This was a big realization for me. When things started to go wrong for me with football, I became really concerned about what people thought about me. I spent a lot of time hiding out in my parents' house and a lot of time partying. In both cases, I was running away from the opinions of others. But eventually I realized that there was no way to run away from this. I couldn't keep people from judging me, because people are *always* judging. What I had to do instead was give them something great to judge. I decided that I wasn't going to allow my voice to be silenced. I wasn't going to lead myself into a deeper depression simply because I was afraid of being judged by the world. And once I decided that, I realized that these bad chapters in my life, these storms I'd experienced, actually created something powerful in my life, something I could use to turn things around. When I look back now, I realize that all of the things I complained about and was ashamed of and wasn't proud of turned me into a man that others became proud of. My bad chapters led me directly to my great chapters.

That was a major breakthrough for me, and it can be a major breakthrough for you too. The minute you accept that others are going to judge you no matter what you do and that there's no hiding from it—they'll just judge you for hiding if you try to hide—then the fear of being judged starts to break down. At that point, you can start looking at your bad chapters—the parts of the story where things are not going well for you as the hero—and start authoring the great chapters that are going to turn the story in your favor.

Owning Your Darkest Moments

If you've seen the movie *8 Mile*, then you'll remember the great rap battle at the end between Eminem's character, Jimmy, and Anthony Mackie's character, Papa Doc. Papa Doc was the most fearsome rapper in the tournament, and he had a plan for taking Jimmy down by bringing up all of the humbling things from Jimmy's life—where Jimmy lived, how he'd messed up in the past, how much trouble he'd had getting ahead. But Jimmy got the jump on him by owning up to all of these things in his own rap, leaving Papa Doc disarmed and without a backup plan. To me, that battle is a great analogy for how to deal with your darkest moments and the worst chapters in your life. When you own these things, when you acknowledge the struggles you've had and might still be having, you get a couple of important things out of the way.

The first is that you make it much harder for other people to use those things against you. If people are out to hurt you or are being a roadblock for you (we're going to get into this a lot more in a few chapters), one of their biggest weapons is your fear of being exposed. They believe that they have some kind of power over you, because you're ashamed of your past or your current situation. But when you own up to it, when you talk about things openly and acknowledge that you have stuff to work on, these people have no power over you. In the movie, Jimmy was always ashamed that he lived in a trailer, and he went out of his way to keep people from finding out that he did. That gave the people who were working against him the power to keep him down. But once he acknowledged his living conditions, any attack using that information lost all of its juice.

The other thing that happens when you own your darkest moments is that you begin to understand something critical for your growth: your struggles and your history don't define you. This is one of the most important things I can say to you here. You *are not* your bad chapters. Your bad chapters are something that happened to you, maybe even something you participated in creating. But they are not you. They are no more you than the clothes you wore yesterday or what you had for dinner a week ago. You are so much more than your bad chapters. You are a complex set of feelings, emotions, dreams, opinions, abilities, and more. Your bad chapters might be dominating your story right now, but they are not who you are at the core. That person is someone with the potential to set all of those bad chapters aside—to own them, to learn from them, and then to move on from them.

Owning your bad chapters is the first step in writing new chapters where the hero triumphs. Own your past, your mistakes, your insecurities, and even your questions about your life and where you are going, and then people can't use these things against you. You'll be amazed at how much stronger you'll feel when you do this. And once you do it, you'll always have that as a tool to work with. You know, people still try to bring up who I used to be and what I used to do when things were going badly for me. They'll point to some stuff that's out there on social media from my bad chapters and try to embarrass me or hurt me. They'll tell me I'm not qualified for my position because of my past. "How can you talk about this when you used to do that?" "How can you talk about being a good man when you weren't a good man?" It's a common thing for people from your past to do—to make who you *were* who you *are*. You have to understand that these people don't know you; they knew you. I refuse to let people make me feel insecure about my growth because of my past. And you have to do the same.

The reason I can get past people talking to me this way is that I owned that stuff a long time ago, which is obvious since I'm speaking openly about these things in this book. So when someone brings any of this stuff up, I have a ready answer: "Right. And look at me now. Isn't God good?" That shuts things down right away. I'm going to help you get to that place.

And here's the other important thing to remember about owning your struggles: everybody struggles. There isn't a single person out there who doesn't have things in their life they wished had turned out differently, or events that went badly, or traits that have created problems for them. I will go so far as to say that there are very few people walking around who don't have at least one thing happening in their lives right now that they wish they could change. Some of these people may be way better at hiding it than others, but they're all carrying around something. The fact that you're dealing with some stuff doesn't make you an exception; it makes you part of the overwhelming majority. The next time you're out in public, look at the people around you and imagine what's going on in their heads. We're *all* feeling bad about something in some way. So you don't have to be perfect for imperfect people. And others shouldn't expect you to be perfect, because they all have their own imperfections to deal with.

If you're dedicating a lot of time and energy to hiding from the reality of imperfections, you're using up precious time and energy that could be put to much better use. You're worrying about being judged, and you're comparing yourself negatively to people who probably have as many bad chapters in their lives as you have in yours. Get rid of that tendency, and you'll find that building from the foundation this pain has provided becomes a lot more realistic.

Your Pain Has a Purpose

People constantly say things to me like, "Everything is going wrong in my life" and "Nothing is right." I get it. I understand how you might feel that way at any given time, if you've hit a bad patch or things aren't going the way you expected or if you haven't reached the place in your life you thought you would by now. But when we say things like that, we forget that we can't see what the future holds. In truth, sometimes things have to "go wrong" to make things go right. It certainly took a lot of things going wrong in my life to bring me to the place I am now. Sometimes going in the "wrong direction" actually leads you to the right place. Maybe "wrong" isn't wrong at all; maybe it's just a different path that you have to take. Sometimes things have to turn out in a way that you don't want them to so that your future can turn out better. Maybe something didn't work out because something else is in the process of working out at a whole other level. Maybe a particular thing had to go "wrong" to push you to a place that you never would have gone if the first thing had worked out "right." Had it succeeded, maybe you never would have gone where you needed to go.

Of course, these "wrong" things come with pain, so let's talk about pain for a while. Lots of people are afraid of pain and will do anything they can to avoid it. They'll avoid uncomfortable situations to stay away from emotional pain. They'll avoid going to the dentist to stay away from physical pain. They won't do what they know they're supposed to do to stay in shape because they don't want the aches and pains that come with it.

But pain has a purpose, and that purpose has an extremely big impact on your life. Pain basically does two things for you. The first is it shows you what's dangerous. If a kid picks up a piece of broken glass and gets cut, the physical pain tells him that he shouldn't do that anymore or that he should at least be more careful if he does it again. Similarly, if you go on a rant online and start saying things about other people that they don't deserve, the response you're going to get from your community is likely to cause you some emotional pain. That pain will send the message that you have to think twice before going off on social media. Pain is one of the strongest indicators that we're in a bad place and that if we continue in it, we're going to be in real trouble. It hurts, and that's a very good thing, because when something hurts, you pay attention to it.

The other thing that pain does for you is to show you that you're getting stronger. This is something that athletes learn at a young age. When you're working as hard as you can on a practice field, you're going to go home every day feeling all kinds of pain. Your body is sending you a powerful message here, and it's a great one—it's telling you that you're pushing your body to new heights. And as anyone who's ever worked out really hard knows, the same level of work isn't going to cause the same level of pain in the long run. Eventually your body will adjust (at which point you'll want to keep pushing harder, but that's another conversation). The same is true of your emotions. People sometimes talk about going outside of their comfort zone. Most of us like to stay where we're comfortable, because we usually don't feel any emotional pain there. We're going to talk about this a lot more later, but the reason staying in your comfort zone is a bad idea is that there's only so much you can accomplish by continuing to do the things you've always done. I know; going *outside* of your comfort zone is painful, right? Definitely, as anyone knows who has ever tried to master new skills, meet new people, or try new projects. It can hurt—in the short run. But just as the workout pain decreases the more you push yourself physically, the same goes for your emotions. And you get a big prize when you do these things: you grow as a person.

So, let me make something clear to you right now: there's no strength without pain. You don't accomplish anything big in life without getting to the point where you think you're going to break down. There's no breakthrough unless you push yourself close to a breakdown. I don't know of any way around it. This doesn't mean that you have to live in crisis mode all the time. That's not healthy, either. Athletes have rest days or days when they scale back their training. People don't go out of their comfort zones every single day; they establish a new, bigger, comfort zone for a while and then push outside of that. But feeling a crisis coming on isn't automatically a sign that you should retreat. First you need to ask yourself if this is a sign that you're experiencing a period of growth. Is the pain that you're feeling an indication that you're actually getting closer to where you want to be? Take a careful look at that, because if it is, then you need to keep pushing through the pain.

And that takes me back to the bad chapters in your life. Now would be a really good time to take a closer look at those bad chapters, even if doing so brings up some unhappy memories. Your bad chapters always come with a lot of pain. They wouldn't be bad otherwise. Let's examine that pain, though. Was it the kind of pain that told you that you were doing something dangerous and that you'd better stop or things were going to get much, much worse? That's probably true in at least some people's cases, like maybe a bad relationship that got really ugly.

But are you finding any situations in your bad chapters where the pain you were feeling might have been a sign of growth? Maybe it hurt so much when you got fired from that job because you weren't quite ready for a job like that, but you were well on the way to acquiring the skills. What would have happened if, instead of ending your search for work in that area, you had gotten more training and then tried again? Could the pain have actually been a message that you just needed to do a few more reps?

I want you to make an agreement with me right here. I want you to commit to seeing pain in a new way, as a super-important message delivery system. If someone were trying to get an important message to you, would it make sense for you to run away from the messenger? Of course not. So listen to the pain and learn what it is telling you. If you can do that, I'll keep showing you ways to take those messages and use them to grow and to become the best possible version of you.

Your Current Situation Is Not Your Final Destination

If you're reading this book, you've either experienced some bad chapters in your life or are in the middle of a bad chapter right now. I know how tough that is, and I know how difficult it is to turn the page on these bad chapters. When I was in the middle of all of my stuff, I thought I was going to be living one bad chapter after another for the rest of my life. But here's the absolute truth: where you are right now is not your final destination.

This is something that Rehabber Rachel needed to learn, and she figured it out in a surprising way. Rachel's bad chapters started when she got married in her late twenties. The man verbally, emotionally, and sexually abused her, leaving her in a place where she was taking her pain and frustration out on her kids and "sleeping around, thinking that if I gave my body away, I would be loved." She'd started to believe that she didn't have any worth and that her story was destined to end badly. She needed to make a change if she was to ever get past the bad chapters. And she went after that change through a surprising source.

Even though she wasn't an alcoholic and had never had any substance abuse issues, Rachel started attending Alcoholics Anonymous meetings. This had a huge effect on her life.

"I went to seven meetings and I agreed to go to a retreat. Wow! The second-hardest thing I ever had to do," she told me. "It was like looking in the mirror, looking at yourself and realizing that you *are* good enough. I was so used to hearing I was worth nothing. I started to accept that I have done wrong, that I have hurt people and have made mistakes, and I started to learn to forgive myself and forgive others. You see, it was so easy to point the finger at others—until I realized there is no one to blame. Of course, you can't fix other people, but you sure as heck can fix yourself."

Those meetings were like the start of a new "act" in the book of Rachel's life. It was time to put the bad chapters behind her. It isn't always easy, but she's creating a great story for herself.

"The hardest thing is to stand in front of the mirror and look at yourself," she says, "to reach deep down inside yourself and really feel the things that have hurt you—feel it completely and cry. Fall to the ground and say, 'God, I put my life in Your hands.' Really feel and understand your pain and learn to cure yourself. I have bad days when I just want to run away, when I cry alone in my room. But when you learn how to look at things differently, you can appreciate and love the darkness as much as the light. The yin and the yang. The not-so-pretty parts of us—the pain and the mistakes— all teach us a lesson. And all the joy, all the happiness, and the wonderful feelings we have teach us that it was all worth it. Even your food tastes better, the sky is more beautiful, and your children's smiles are your most precious treasure."

Rachel was once so deep in her pain that it must have seemed to her that she could never get past it. But here's the thing about any situation you find yourself in: you can definitely move on from it. You will definitely get to the next chapter of your life. The only question is how that chapter is going to read. So work to make it a chapter where the hero begins to triumph.

If you're like a lot of people, when things are going well, you're worried that the good times are going to end. But when things are going badly, you think it's going to be like this forever. I don't know why, but that's the way most of us think. But if you really look back on your life, you'll see that both the good stuff and the bad stuff eventually moved on. That's the way life works. You do have some level of control over this, of course. If you allow yourself to get caught up in feeling miserable about the bad stuff, you can make it last a lot longer than it should. And if you learn from what you experience when things are going well, you can make the bad times nothing more than the occasional annoyance or learning experience.

That's what I want us to work on together now. I know we've been talking mostly about bad chapters here, but I want you to take a little time to think about the best chapters in your life so far. Why were those periods in your life so good? What was working for you? Who were you with? What were you spending most of your time doing?

I realize not all of us can reproduce the circumstances of our best chapters. Things change. Maybe those chapters included someone who died or moved far away, so that person is no longer available. Maybe they came during your childhood, and we all know you can't go back to that. Maybe you were in a relationship that ended. But even in situations where circumstances changed, it wasn't just those external forces that made those times so good—it was also *you*! Who were *you* during those "good times"? Were you more open to taking chances? Were you more innocent? Were you more willing to make a leap of faith?

I think if you really give this some thought, you'll realize that the best chapters of your life involve something about you that you were particularly satisfied with, some trait that is part of the very best version of you. How can you get yourself back to that? Yeah, that relationship is long over, and he turned out to be kind of a jerk in the end, but how did it feel to have your heart so open and to be receptive enough to love in the first place? You certainly can't go back to being five years old again, but is there something about the way you took in the world back then that you can recapture? Identifying the best parts of your best times is one valuable way to bring those best times back.

Now, let's go back to those bad chapters. First of all, let's put something important on the table: only in the most extreme cases are your worst situations 100 percent terrible. I know those situations exist, and if you've been in one of them, I can truly sympathize. For the most part, though, even when things are going really badly, there's still some good stuff going on. Maybe it's one great friend or family member who's always there for you even when everything is falling apart. Maybe it's a sport or a hobby that gives you a few hours off from your troubles. Maybe it's music or a pet or just a walk around the neighborhood. It's important to keep this in mind both because it's a reminder that even your worst times include some good and because what is good during your worst times is stuff that you can focus on during your best times.

But now let's look at that worst stuff. First, remember that even if you're currently in the middle of some of your worst circumstances ever, this is not your final destination, and between these tough times and better days, you are growing. Now, consider this: plants don't grow without rain. Yeah, storms suck, but those downpours in your life are a necessary part of your growing. The rain is going to end, and when the sun comes back out, you're going to have more of what you need to get bigger and better.

Sometimes an "inability" can lead to your greatest ability. That's what happened to me when my struggle to make it in football led to my creation of RehabTime, which brought me to where I am now. In my case, my inability to succeed at my dream was causing me to throw everything I had into my desire for something that I couldn't have. It nearly took me out. But then I started working on ways to fix myself, and that got me to sharing some of those methods with others, and that led me to my greatest ability, which is inspiring people and helping them to be who they really want to be. When I was weighed down by my inability, I was living through the worst chapters of my entire life. But that very inability and the way I dealt with it led me right to my greatest ability.

The same thing can happen for you. Once you convince yourself that the worst times are most definitely going to pass, you can use the process of getting out of those worst times to lead you to something great.

Falling in Love with the Progression

If you're really going to turn the page on your bad chapters and have your story turn out great, you need to feel good about the process of getting to that best place and accept that it doesn't happen instantly or without a few complications. I call this "falling in love with the progression." Think about it. If you need to lose a lot of weight, it isn't all going to come off in a couple of days. There might even be a period where you stop losing weight or even gain a little back. If you're fixing up an old house, it's going to take months, and there are going to be times when the house looks worse than it did when you started. If you're learning a new skill, you're not going to become an expert overnight, and there may even be times when you feel like you're getting worse at it rather than better. That's the way nearly every progression works. Some good days—hopefully, lots of them—and definitely some bad. The key is to love all of it, because the progression is getting you where you want to go.

The people who succeed at improving their lives do so because they realize that if they have a good plan and commit to sticking to it, they've already started winning. Being on the plan feels so right, and they love the progression so much that they truly embrace the path they're on. As we get further along in this book, I'm going to give you lots of tools to use to put together a great plan, but before we can get there, I want you to understand that loving the execution of that plan is the key to its success. You have to enjoy this experience. If you go into it with a ton of skepticism or if you're ready to quit as soon as something goes wrong, you're just not going to get where you want to go.

And let me be clear about something: not every day is going to be great. Doctors say that one of the big challenges for patients is that when they start to fix a chronic problem, the first sign of healing is increased pain. That's because nerve endings that have been shut down for a long time begin coming back to life and they let you know that you've got some damage there. You've probably had at least some experience with this yourself. Did you ever notice that the day after you get a cut, it often hurts more than it did when the cut first happened? That's because the nerves first shut down in response to the pain, but then as you start healing, the nerves go back to normal and start to ache a little. When that pain comes, though, you probably don't panic. You don't tell yourself that if the cut hurts on the second day, it is getting worse and you need to get yourself to the emergency room. You might check to make sure nothing is infected, but you know that the cut is on its way to getting better; it's just a matter of time, and you're doing what you need to do to make sure your cut is going to heal.

That's the way it's going to be when you start to turn the page on your bad chapters. Even if you have a great plan and your progression is going really well, some annoying and even upsetting stuff is going to happen. Maybe somebody from the old life you're trying to get away from says something about you on social media, and you suddenly feel the way you did when things were going badly. Maybe you're doing a great job of staying away from your addiction, but one day you just want it *so much*. Maybe you've been doing really well at improving your sense of self-worth, but you get a flash of doubt, and then you don't feel as good about yourself. Any of these things can throw you off and make you feel that you're going to fail. But remember that falling in love with the progression is all about loving what you're doing for yourself, even when part of it involves some pain and some setbacks. Pull back, remind yourself where the progression has taken you already, and then tell yourself that while the pain is only temporary, the progression is permanent.

It's not healthy to always focus on the destination because it can be discouraging to see how far you actually have to go. Sometimes it makes you forget how far you have actually come! That's why falling in love with the progression is crucial in your journey because it gives you a sense of both aspects. You see how far you've come, and when you do, this breathes new energy into your life to continue the journey.

My mother knows a ton about making her way through the journey, because she went through a very powerful journey of her own. In the spring of 2017, she was diagnosed with stage 4 cancer in her breast and liver. Her doctor told her that she had large masses in both places as well as "fifteen or more" (he wouldn't be more specific) other masses in her body—all malignant. Her oncologist told her that if she didn't do any treatments, she would have between six and nine months to live, at the same time making her aware that even if she did the treatment, there weren't any guarantees.

My mother knew she was in for the biggest challenge of her life, but she had it in her to trust the progression.

"There's a scripture that I've always held on to," she told me. And then she paraphrased Psalm 112:7. "'I do not fear bad news or evil tidings, because I know that my heart is fixed, and I trust in God. Therefore, I will not be afraid.' Whenever

I hear news that is not good news, I always go to that scripture. I was concerned, of course, but I was not afraid."

At the same time, she was going through tremendous pain. She told me it was "worse than natural childbirth. It was the most horrendous pain I have ever experienced, and I have a good tolerance for pain." She started to wonder if she would be around for Thanksgiving or Christmas, while at the same time refusing to count six to nine months forward from April, because she didn't want to think in those terms.

Mom had a good support system and her faith, which made a huge difference.

"The support of my family was just outstanding. It's very important that you have positive reinforcement, especially from your immediate family. I had that. You also have to encourage yourself. There were days when I didn't get a phone call, or a text, or a knock on the door with flowers. On those days, I knew I could not depend on anyone else but myself and Jesus."

But despite her faith, and despite her support system, and despite her being convinced that she was going to get to the other side of cancer, there were still some very bad days. Maybe the worst of these were when her hair started coming out, because "no woman wants to lose her hair. When my hair came out, I felt horrible; I felt ugly; I felt ashamed. I felt less than." My barber, Jeremy, wound up being a big help here, finding a way to leave her with a little bit of her hair and also talking with her and praying with her. When she was going through this disease, with all of its other complications, she could have given up on the progression, given up on her ultimate goal, but instead she kept powering through.

"I've learned in all situations to give thanks, for that is the will of God. When I found out [I had cancer], my first words were, 'Okay, God, I don't like this. I don't understand this. I don't know why You have allowed me to go through this, but I'm thanking You. Because in the end, You're gonna get the glory and I'm gonna be much better for it.' I always knew I was not going to die. I knew it was going to be a struggle. I knew it wasn't going to be pleasant. But I did know that I was not going to die."

On October 31, 2017, my mother went to the doctor to get the results of a PET scan that would show what was happening with the cancer all over her body. And that's when she learned that her falling in love with the progression had paid off.

"My oncologist looked at his screen and he leaned forward, then sat back and said, 'These are dramatic and unusual results. Mrs. Shelton, there is no evidence of disease in your body.' I always knew I was going to be healed, but I didn't think it would come in only six months of treatment. I said, 'What are you saying to me?' He repeated it three or four times. Then I reached over, took his face in my hands, and drew him in to me. And I'm crying at that point. 'What are you saying to me?' I said again, and he said, 'Mrs. Shelton, you have no cancer in your body.' Those were the words that I had been waiting on. Those were the words on those horrible down days that I would just imagine would be said to me. To finally hear those words was surreal. I jumped up out of my chair and I got on my knees in the middle of my doctor's office, and I went into total praise, thanking God for what He had done.

"Since going through this, I see things differently than I ever did before. Some things I thought were so important are not, and some things I thought were not so important are, and I don't take anything for granted. When I wake up, I'm like, 'Thank You, Lord. Thank You, Jesus. I have another day.' I can help someone. I can give someone hope. I can tell someone, 'This is what happened to me.' I consider myself to be a miracle. Now, doctors may consider 'miracle' to be a strong word, but when you go from six to nine months to live to being completely cancer-free, I consider that to be a miracle.

"Not everybody is chosen to go through such a horrible journey. So, my God must see something in me that I'm not even aware of. I'm not patting myself on the back, because who wants to go through almost losing their life? But I'm just amazed and thankful. If I had to do this over again, I would do it, because I'm a much better person for this, and I'm going to be a much better person through this, because I'm going to be able to help other people. I've walked in those shoes, I've been through that journey, and I'm completely healed and saved and delivered. I'm free like I've never been free before."

When my mom was in her cancer battle, I told her to not focus on being healed. I didn't want her to think that just because she wasn't healed yet, she wasn't healing. I told her to focus on the *process* of healing. Every part of her journey was healing. Losing her hair? Healing. Losing weight? Healing. All of it was healing. I constantly reminded her that, yes, the progression sucks, but the progression is necessary.

I think the miracle she experienced had an awful lot to do with falling in love with the progression. And while you might never go through anything as dramatic or life-threatening as she did, falling in love with the progression can deliver the same kind of results to you.

A Few Questions Before Moving On

I hope you're with me on this now and you know that your bad chapters aren't your whole story and that they definitely aren't an indication of where your story is going to wind up in the long run. No matter what you've gone through, you can still make things turn out right. That's what we're going to be working on together for the rest of this book.

Before we get there, though, take a look at these questions and give some serious thought to the answers. I know I don't really need to remind you again, but let me just say one more time that you've got to answer these questions with absolute honesty.

- What were or are the bad chapters in your life?
- Are you ready to own those bad chapters?
- Do you see pain as a message or something to be avoided at all costs?
- Do you think where you are right now is where you're going to be forever?
- Are you ready to embrace everything—even the occasional painful parts—about making your progression?

We're dealing with a lot of big stuff here. What's important is that you not say, "Yeah, Trent, I get it. Let's get to the plan." You don't want to pass through this until you're really convinced that turning the page on your bad chapters is something that you yourself can do. I'm about to throw some very big challenges at you, so you're going to need all the strength that comes when you finally accept that you can put your bad chapters behind you.

4

BURNING BRIDGES

I've already shared some pretty serious stories about my life in this book, and trust me, I have more to come. But I want to start this chapter by making myself look bad over something a little lighter—my wife loves to laugh about it—that still taught me a valuable lesson.

A few years ago, my family and I moved into a new house, and we wanted the backyard to look great, so we got a fire pit and a bunch of other stuff to make it a place where people could come to protect their peace. Once we had that all set up, my wife looked around and said that she thought that things could look even better if we did a little landscaping near the fire pit. I told her I thought that was a really good idea, and she said she'd make a few calls in the morning.

"No," I said. "I can do this."

She looked at me funny, because gardening wasn't exactly

a skill I'd shown proficiency at. I might have brought her flowers on any number of occasions, but I sure didn't plant the flowers that I gave her.

"You're gonna do this," she said.

"Yeah, I can do it."

I knew she wasn't convinced, but I had confidence in myself. *How hard could it be? I'll just enroll in YouTube University and become a self-proclaimed professional gardener overnight.* (Hey, I know a lot of you reading this book have taken a few classes on YouTube.) So the next day, I went to the nursery, not mentioning to my wife that at first I thought a nursery was a place you find babies, not plants. When I got there, my pride caused me to pretend like I knew what I was looking for. I needed help, but I sure wasn't going to ask for it. After about ten minutes of watching me looking confused, a salesperson insisted on helping me. I'm sure he could tell I was lost. I told him what I was looking to do, and he showed me a bunch of plants that he thought would work well in that situation. I didn't ask any questions; I just bought what looked good to me.

Then I went home and planted them. Just dug holes in the ground and stuck them in. I didn't think about the kind of soil I was putting these plants in or whether I needed to do anything to that soil. I didn't think about the fact that it was the middle of the summer in Texas and that these plants were probably going to need a crazy amount of water if they stood any chance at all. I didn't even think about how deep the holes needed to be. I just dug in until it looked like the plants would fit, stuck the plants in the ground, and moved the dirt back around them. I'm pretty sure I sprayed some water on them afterward, but I certainly didn't make a habit of watering these things in the following days.

When I was finished, I stepped back and admired my work. The plants looked great around the fire pit. And they kept looking great for a few days. Then they started to die.

My first thought was that the guy at the nursery had sold me a bunch of bad plants, so I went back there and told him what had happened. He asked me to explain exactly what I did after I brought the plants home, so I did.

"Yeah, you did it totally wrong," he said after I'd finished.

He then went on to explain to me about evaluating the soil, understanding the positioning of the plants, and about the best time of year for planting certain kinds of plants in this area. He mentioned that watering was kind of important. He brought up a few other things, but by this point, all I was hearing was, "You are not handy at all."

I left the nursery with some more stuff and did what I thought I could handle myself. Then I hired a professional to do the rest of the job.

I try to look for lessons in everything, and this was definitely a learning experience. I'm big on taking responsibility and on self-accountability, so the first thing I thought about was how, if I were going to do any job, I had to put in the time to figure out how to do it right. That message seems pretty obvious, right?

But then I started looking at this from the plants' perspective. When that first batch of plants died, my first thought was to blame the plants. They didn't grow, so they must have been bad plants. I said as much to the guy at the nursery when I went back to complain. But in reality, those plants never stood a chance because the environment they were in gave them no chance. They were put in the hands of a guy who knew so little about gardening that he didn't even realize how little he knew about gardening. From the time I bought those plants, all the odds were against them.

And then I realized that all of us sometimes find ourselves in the same situation. We're in an environment where there's no chance we can grow, because that environment makes growth impossible. My gardening disaster reminded me of a tweet by Alexander Den Heijer I saw awhile back: "When a flower doesn't bloom, you fix the environment in which it grows, not the flower." Thinking about it again really drove home a point. How many times have you blamed yourself or have other people blamed you for not being the best version of you when what is really to blame is your situation? Is it you who is failing to grow, or is it everything around you that is giving you no possible chance of growing?

The plants around my fire pit had no chance from the minute I bought them. They didn't have a say in who their gardener was, and they couldn't take a look at the conditions and say, "You know what? I'm out of here." Fortunately, the same isn't true for you. If you're in a terrible situation—if the people you're with or the relationships you're in are giving you as little chance of being everything you can be as I gave that first batch of plants—you have the power to change things. You may not think that you do, but you do. It might not be easy, and it will come with some pain, but you can absolutely get yourself out of the situations that prevent you from growing. The next step in our process is how to do exactly that.

Where Your Bridges Lead You

I'm gonna switch up the metaphor now. The gardening story is a really good illustration, but now that I've finished telling stories on myself and we're ready to roll up our sleeves and get to work, I think there's a symbol that can be more instructive. Let's talk about bridges.

Bridges take us across territory that is tough to cross otherwise. Unless you're a really good swimmer or you have an awesome all-terrain vehicle, in some situations a bridge is just about the only way to get from one point to another. But bridges don't offer any guidance about their destination. There's nobody on one end of a bridge stopping you and saying, "Yeah, you can cross, but have you thought hard about what's on the other side and whether you really want to go there?"

We have all kinds of bridges in our personal lives. There are social bridges, groups of people who lead us to a certain kind of lifestyle. There are relationship bridges that lead us to different levels of intimacy. There are professional bridges that lead us toward the futures of our careers. There are family and community bridges that lead us to a particular place in the world, with a particular set of expectations and potentials.

Really, if you look at every connection you have in the world, each connection is a bridge of one kind or another. The big question, though, is whether that particular bridge is taking you toward the greatest you, or a lesser you.

It isn't always easy to tell the difference. It isn't just about how crossing a particular bridge makes you feel. For example, a bridge can lead you into a social situation where you're going out all the time and life is one big party. That feels pretty good, but if you do it for too long, it becomes destructive and could cause you to regress as a person. In a minute, I'll tell you about how that happened to me. Meanwhile, a different bridge might lead you to a relationship in which you have a lot of things to work out and a lot of difficult decisions to make. That might not feel great at all, but the hard work you're doing when you cross that bridge is making you stronger and better. It's making you more of the person you really want to be and getting you closer to being the greatest you. That's a good bridge even if it doesn't always make you feel good.

Now's the time for another exercise for you to be straight up with yourself. I want you to think about every bridge you have in your life—every connection that takes you from where you are on your own to a place with other people, other circumstances, and other situations. Now think about where that bridge is really leading you.

If it's a good bridge, it's leading you to a place where you're supported, where you're challenged, where you're given every opportunity to grow and get better. Maybe you have a bridge that takes you to a friend or a group of friends who always have your back, who really believe in you but also let you know when you're messing up. That sounds like a great bridge. Maybe you have a bridge to a church where the pastor regularly inspires you and you walk away feeling ready to take positive steps in your life. That's a great one too.

But then there are the bad bridges. A bad bridge ultimately leads to pain and regression, no matter how you're feeling when you cross that bridge. Maybe you have a bridge to a relationship that sometimes makes you happy but often leaves you feeling inadequate or less than. The bridge's ultimate destination is a whole lot of hurt. Maybe you have a bridge to a community of people who put you down or tell you that your dreams are worthless. There's no chance that bridge is taking you to your best self.

Sometimes, it isn't all that easy to tell if a bridge leads to a good place or a bad one. Maybe that group of friends offers you lots of support, but they also enable certain self-destructive tendencies, like settling for less or ignoring your flaws. That group might want the best for you, but they're actually not helping you achieve your best. On the other hand, maybe that relationship that often leaves you feeling small actually just requires a serious conversation to turn it into a good bridge. Your partner might not even realize how he's making you feel, and once you clear the air, it turns out that he's ready to give you what you really need.

So, when you're thinking about all of your bridges, you need to answer this question with as much clarity as you can: Is this bridge leading me on the road to pain? If the answer is yes, it's probably time to burn that bridge.

Knowing When It's Time to Burn Bridges

It took Rehabber Cheri a little time to get to her answer. She met a guy in high school, and their relationship quickly evolved from friendship to romance. There were some red flags in the relationship right from the start, like the fact that he was regularly talking behind her back and showing her a general lack of respect. But as Cheri describes it, they were in their "honeymoon" phase, and she was also "innocent and a little naive," so she overlooked these things.

But the longer they were together, the more the negative behavior started to outweigh the positive. "He was mean and manipulative," she told me. "He never wanted to hang out with me anymore. He only wanted to be with friends, and he would blow me off and call me clingy and annoying for wanting to spend time with him. This is when I started to become really insecure both as a person as well as in the relationship. I began to feel like I just wasn't enough. Being constantly told that I was annoying and crazy solely because I wanted to be around him was starting to take a toll on me. His emotional abuse literally made me feel like I was a bad person."

Cheri and her boyfriend started arguing all the time, and eventually he broke up with her. A week later, though, they were back together. "I was really vulnerable and in love, so as soon as he would apologize to me (no matter how superficial it was), I would take him back instantly."

What followed were three years of the same, repeated pattern. Cheri's boyfriend would treat her badly and make her feel awful, and then he'd do something to make her stick around. But he kept leading her back to manipulation and abuse, and he was so good at it that Cheri let herself take the blame. "I would try to express my feelings in a way he'd understand and respect, but I never got anything in return. Instead of being sincere and listening to me about where I was coming from, he simply wouldn't care. He would actually flip the situation on me, calling me crazy, annoying, clingy, etc. He'd claim that I wasn't a good girlfriend because I didn't trust him. Each and every time he did this, I started to truly believe him. I'd start to believe that maybe he was right, and maybe I wasn't being a good girlfriend."

Cheri was in a very bad place, but she couldn't make herself give up on the relationship. "It was hard to think about letting him go after all that we'd been through. It was even harder imagining my life without him. I would let the good outweigh the bad, although looking back, the bad always outweighed the good. It was the same pattern again and again, and no matter how much I wanted not to forgive him, I always did. I would cave each and every time."

After three years, this bridge had led Cheri somewhere she never wanted to go and the on-again, off-again relationship was off again. "I was completely broken, and I questioned every day how someone I was so good to, who said he loved me, who I gave my all to, could up and leave me without looking back? He was a damaged person whom I spent an enormous amount of time trying to fix. I never gave up on him. I took the verbal and emotional abuse. I took being treated less than what I deserved, and I ate up every single lie he would tell me. There wasn't one thing that I wouldn't have done for him. It eventually came to a point where I had lost myself. I wasn't hanging out with my friends and family anymore, I was miserable all the time, I couldn't concentrate in my daily life, and I was constantly worrying about what my boyfriend was doing. I was a completely different person, someone I truly did not recognize anymore."

It was at this point that Cheri began speaking to her father, a devout Christian, about God. She started praying every night for guidance and took to heart her father's advice that she "ignore all the daily distractions and truly open my heart up." This led to the breakthrough Cheri desperately needed. She finally saw that the bridge between herself and her boyfriend was leading her to a life of pain and humiliation—and that it was time to burn it. By replacing her dependency on the relationship with faith in God, Cheri gained the strength to burn a bridge that badly needed burning.

"I have built a relationship with God; I seek Him often and pray to Him every night. I'm finally free and I am so happy. I am finding myself again, and I'm turning over a new leaf. I finally realized that I can't keep going back to what broke me. It's been seven months since the breakup, and my ex is currently trying to reenter my life. But for the first time, I finally have the power and the strength to say no. I know I deserve better."

As Cheri's story illustrates, burning a bridge is a huge deal, and none of us want to take that sort of thing lightly. Maybe the bridge is to a group of people you've known since you were a kid. Maybe it's to someone who once meant an awful lot in your life. These aren't the kinds of people you let go of easily, and the last thing you want to do is burn a bridge when it isn't necessary to do so.

But how do you know? The first question to ask is this: Is this person draining me? Let's talk about that a little. When someone is draining you, he or she is killing your emotional energy. A draining relationship is one where, no matter how you're feeling before you're with that person, you feel worse afterward. This is not always easy to diagnose. For example, you may laugh a lot and feel in high spirits while you're together, but at the end of the night or the next morning, you feel worn out or depressed or even a little ashamed. Does that happen a lot when you're with this person? If so, that person is draining you. Or maybe you spend time with someone who has deep heart-to-heart talks with you, where you get into a lot of heavy stuff, but these conversations always leave you feeling less optimistic about life. The intimacy of these conversations might be exciting, but that person is draining you.

People who drain you might not even realize they're doing it. They might not be actively trying to hurt you, but they're still hurting you. For whatever reason, that relationship is toxic for you, and you're not going to be able to grow as long as you stay in that toxic environment. It's like my gardening story. The soil I was putting the plants in wasn't "evil" soil. It was just the wrong soil for those plants, and unless I changed the soil, my plants were going to keep dying.

So, the first thing you need to do when you're considering burning a bridge is determine whether you're being drained or not. If you are, then it's time to burn that thing down. That's what happened to me when I was in the middle of my battle to stick with football. I had a bridge to a group of people who I spent a lot of time partying with. By "a lot of time," I mean just about every night. I had a great time while we were at the club, but I slowly realized that this bridge only led to one thing: more partying. I was valuing things I should not have valued and making things a priority I should not have been prioritizing. I was expecting to move my life forward by doing the very things that were holding my life back. Many times I would wake up the next morning feeling awful about how I was living my life, and I'd tell myself that I needed to do something better with it. That cycle was draining me, but I couldn't see it for what it was back then. It really wasn't until my son, Tristan, was born and I realized that I needed to be a better man for him that I could see what this group was doing to me. I was never going to grow as long as I kept going out with these people, so I finally convinced myself to burn that bridge.

Another question to ask yourself when you're looking at your bridges is, where does this end up? This is a question a lot of us never think about when we're considering our relationships. We give too much credit to the early moments. Those early moments give us an emotional high. But where do you see it going? What's the endgame? What's the final page of the story? Often, the damage a relationship is causing us happens slowly and you won't even notice it until it's too late. Maybe that guy you're seeing treats you pretty okay. You don't fight a lot, and you've got a decent rhythm going. Except there's that thing about his always putting down your dreams. You tell him about some ambition you have for your career or for something to do on the side and he patiently explains to you why that's a bad idea. So, how do things end up if you stick with him? They probably end up with you realizing ten years from now that you regret not going after bigger things when you had the chance. Is that something you really want?

Let me go back to that group of people that I needed to cut myself off from. One of the things that convinced me to do it was taking a look at the future. I imagined myself with these people three years, ten years, twenty years down the line, still drinking too much, still taking way too many drugs, still wasting my nights on empty pursuits. When I took an honest look at where I was going with these people, I realized this group wasn't going to evolve into something more nurturing and productive; it was always going to be just what it was. And once I saw where that was going to end up, I knew it had to be over. I had to do way better than that for my son.

At the same time, you could have a bridge that leads you to a group or a relationship that isn't in the best shape and doesn't feel like it's helping you grow. But before you decide to burn that bridge, ask one more question: Is that person or are the people in that group trying to get better? This is an important one for me, because I'm big on taking responsibility and what it means when someone is committed to taking responsibility. Maybe you have a friend who spends your time together talking about her problems. She's got boyfriend problems, she has money problems, she and her sister are always fighting, and she hates her job. You come home after being with this person and feel as if you've just run a marathon, because you're emotionally exhausted. You think that maybe it's time to burn this bridge. But then you think about what your friend has been saying about her situation. She's just about convinced herself to leave the boyfriend; she's watching some videos on YouTube about budgeting her money better; her relationship with her sister is as much a mess as it has ever been, but she's just applied for a new job in her company that she knows she would like a lot more. When you think about it, you realize that she's trying. She might be a long way from getting where she needs to go, and you're probably going to endure a lot more exhausting conversations with her in the future, but she's as interested in working on her life as you're interested in working on yours. Maybe you need to have a conversation with her about shifting the balance of your nights out, but this might be a bridge worth keeping. Maybe this is the kind of person you actually need in your life going forward because she's making a real effort and that effort can keep you inspired.

To get to the greatest you, you're definitely going to need to burn some bridges. By thinking about the issues we've discussed, you'll have a pretty good sense of which bridges those are. Now comes the hard part.

Enduring the Short-Term Pain

Admitting to yourself that you need to burn some bridges takes a lot of guts. Do you want to know what takes even more guts? Actually burning them. This is one of the toughest things you're going to have to do as you go through the process in this book. Even after you know—without a doubt—that you need to cut a person or a group of people out of your life, you're still going to want to avoid doing it. And it's easy to understand why. Very often, bridge burning is a painful experience.

Rehabber Amber avoided dealing with that pain for a long time. As she was growing up, her parents and siblings consistently failed her. "I lived through abuse, parents being in jail, divorce of parents, abandonment, having to parent my sibling and help take care of an alcoholic mother," she told me. "By the time I reached eighteen, I was exhausted, broken, and very depressed about life and what my future would hold."

And yet, even well into her twenties, Amber kept putting up with her family. She tried to convince herself that all families had problems and that the ones in her family weren't all that unusual. Even when she made new friends and met her husband and through these people saw that she deserved better, she stuck with her family.

"For a long time, I felt I had to stay loyal to my family, so I would just try to deal with them in small doses. But as time went on, I kept getting red flag after red flag—although a red flag could have hit me smack in the face, and I still would have tried to unify my family. Something negative would happen to cause me pain by them; I would forgive without any apology, and then pretend like nothing ever happened. Just to keep the peace. I would accept the behavior, vent to my husband about it, cry a lot, and then try to move on. But it just kept repeating over and over. And I began to feel like a fool. They knew they could treat me any way they wanted and I would always be there and forgive."

Amber even forgave her mother for not showing up at her wedding and for ignoring Amber's new baby. Amber knew any break from her family was going to be painful, and as is completely understandable, she tried to avoid that pain.

But then something happened that made it impossible to avoid. Amber's father-in-law was in intensive care for four months, and Amber had a one-year-old, a job, and she needed to go to the hospital every day. She called her mother for help . . . and got no answer.

"If she didn't show up for that . . . what would she be there for?"

Amber had finally gotten to the point where she could no longer worry about the pain of burning a bridge—the bridge had to come down. She cut off all ties to her family and suffered the emotional consequences she knew were coming.

"I let myself grieve. I cried, I tried to read books that I thought could help, I vented and talked to those I trusted, and I searched for pages or support groups online that I thought could help me. Holidays, events, and worst of all, my own birthday were triggers for me."

Burning a bridge that had been there from the beginning of her life was predictably tough for Amber. But now that she's made it through most of the pain, it's obvious to her that she's much better off not going where that bridge had been taking her.

"The pain has lessened day by day, and sometimes I will catch myself thinking, 'Wow, I haven't been upset or even given my family a thought in a while.' I can't even begin to express how good that feels. More peace has entered my life since letting them go, although I know I still have things to heal and work on as I go forward. But I am less broken than I used to be, and I'm healing myself every day. If I had kept them in my life, I would have stayed stuck. I had to mother myself and be my own parent and love myself enough to finally let them go."

We've all had relationships end in an instant. Something gets said, or something gets done, an argument follows, and you cut yourself off from that person. And I'm sure you've also had situations where relationships just fade away—you spend less and less time with someone, and suddenly it's been a few months, and then a year, and then you just lose touch completely. Burning a bridge isn't like either of those scenarios. A bad bridge needs burning only if that bridge is consistently taking you to a place that is harming your growth. Those relationships tend to have lots of layers to them and don't disappear with an argument or just fade over time. For example, if you've spent years with a group that isn't good for you, there are probably a lot of expectations built into your place in that group, and it's going to take some work to untangle yourself. That's how it was with the group I needed to separate myself from when I was still playing football. I was the one who was getting us into the VIP rooms at clubs. I was usually the one paying the check. If I just started not showing up, people would notice. The same is true with one-on-one situations. If you're in a romantic relationship with someone, breaking away usually doesn't happen in a snap. You have plans, you have connections to each other's friends and families, and there might be financial entanglements and even living conditions to deal with.

Getting out of these situations requires work and heartache, and none of that is fun. It's easy to understand why you might convince yourself that hanging in there is better, even when you know for a fact that this bridge needs to come down. Sure, you know it's bad, but is it so bad that you're willing to deal with a nightmare?

If you're thinking that way, let me ask you this: How much do you care about your future? I mean, *really* care. The fact that you're reading this book suggests that you're serious about improving your life, but still, give this question some real thought right now. Is your number one objective to make your future a whole lot better than your past and your present? Maybe when you're thinking just about yourself, you can be a little uncertain about the answer to that question. But what about the other people who are counting on you being the best version of yourself? The big turning point for me was when I realized that the only way I could be a good father to my son and give him what he deserved was to be the best version of myself—and once I came to that realization, I had all the strength I needed to burn the bridges I needed to burn.

What it all comes down to is this: Burning a bridge is a painful experience. There's going to be hurt and ugliness and complications. But if you really care about your future, if you want your future to be much, much better than your present, then you need to accept the fact that the pain associated with burning a bridge is way preferable to the long-term damage you'll suffer if you don't burn that bridge. Think about it like having a bum knee. The knee is causing you pain every single day, but it's not so painful that you can't survive it—at least not right now. You know that surgery can fix the problem, but surgery involves an agonizing rehab process, so you keep avoiding it. But if you don't have that surgery, you're eventually going to have more and more trouble walking, and then the trouble you have walking is going to affect your back, and then the back pain is going to affect other parts of your body, and one day you're not going to be able to get out of bed and it might be too late to clean up all the damage. That's what you have to look at when you worry about the pain associated with burning a bridge. You need to accept that the short-term pain—no matter how intense it is—is better than the long-term pain that will come if you don't make the move.

That's what it came down to for me. I asked myself if I was willing to live the rest of my life the way I'd been living it, and then I thought about my son and realized that that wasn't a future I could accept. Right then, I decided that I would rather go through what I had to go through to burn those bad bridges, because eventually I would find healing and growth and strength. It wasn't going to be easy, but I couldn't afford to live the rest of my life like this.

And so, I went to my party group and I told them that they weren't helping me to become better, so I had to let them go. As you can imagine, I got some pushback on this. Some people said to me, "How can you just get rid of people like that? Where's your loyalty?" And what I realized was that I'm loyal to my principles, not to particular people—and that those who respected my principles would receive my loyalty. I told these people that I could continue to love them from a distance, but that I could not be around them anymore because there were people in my life who depended on me being the best me, and I couldn't let those people down.

Everybody Can Win

In case you're still not completely convinced that the short-term pain of burning a bridge is better than the long-term agony of keeping that bridge up, let me make one more important point. It's very possible that burning your bridge is what *everyone involved* needs. You might be dreading the idea of breaking up a relationship that isn't good for you, but maybe both of you will be able to move on to healthier relationships if you have the strength to move on from this one. Maybe walking away from a group will inspire other people in that group and help them make the kinds of improvements in their lives that you are making in yours, and everyone will come out better as a result.

I've had experience with both of these scenarios. Do you remember the girlfriend I told you about in chapter 1? Our relationship was on again, off again, and sometimes it was great and sometimes it really wasn't. Somewhere deep in my heart, I probably knew that this relationship wasn't good for either of us, but I definitely wasn't acknowledging that, and I certainly wasn't thinking it was time for it to end. Then, one day, she walked out of my life. I guess she finally saw that our future together was not going to play out well for her, and she convinced herself that getting out was the best thing for her future. When she left, I was devastated. I felt rejected and lonely, and in that moment, I couldn't understand why it had happened. Breaking up with me must have been a painful thing for her, and I'm sure it caused her some anguish both just before and right after. But she was right to do it, because we'd gotten to an unhealthy place, and I know her future was better without me than it would have been if we'd stayed together. That breakup really shook me up. But you know what? It also really woke me up. I saw that the breakup happened because I was letting myself get into bad habits, like partying too much and being unfaithful and not making any effort to improve myself. And once I awakened to that fact, I started making the moves that got me to a much better place. It might've never happened if we'd stayed together. So, her burning her bridge with me was the best thing for both of us.

I saw this from the other perspective when I split from that social group I've been telling you about. Before I made the move, I thought long and hard about making it. And telling that group that I couldn't be with them anymore was rough. Some people in the group understood when I said that

I was doing it for my son, but a bunch of others hated the idea that they weren't going to be getting into VIP rooms or rubbing elbows with famous people anymore. I had to face some serious anger and criticism, and that was not easy to take. When people would challenge me about it, I would just say, "We can't hang out like we used to. I'll be there if you need me, but I have to work on me. I have to step away and go into my little cocoon, so I can be better." That didn't always help, but a fascinating thing happened over time: some of the people in that group not only started to understand why I'd needed to step away from them, but they gained some inspiration from the work I was doing. They looked at where they were and compared it to where they wanted to be, and they started working on their own lives. They saw that I was much happier and in a much healthier place, and they wanted some of that for themselves, so they did some of the work that I'd been doing, and it made a real difference. A couple of the people from that group are back in my life now, and the new relationship we have is so much stronger and healthier than the previous one was, because they've struggled and pushed themselves, and their lives have matured because of it.

You can find yourself in exactly this situation if you have the courage to burn bridges that need to be burned. You know it's the best thing for you. If you've done the work that we did earlier in this chapter, you've already decided that you can't be the best version of yourself as long as a particular bridge is still standing. But it also might very well be the best thing for everyone involved. Other people might need that bridge to be burned as much as you do, but they just can't see it or they're just not strong enough to do what has to be done. When you

THE GREATEST YOU

make the move for them, you could be starting a process that gets *them* where they need to go—and might even get them back in your life at some point, this time with a bridge that leads to growth.

So while there's no getting around the fact that burning bridges is a hard thing to do, bringing with it pain and some very difficult days, there are benefits to doing it that go even further than the improvements it makes to your own life. Think about that as you start to light the fire to bring down that bridge. That fire might also light a spark in others that leads them on their own better paths.

And there's a final point I want to make here: a bridge is not a person. The bridge you're burning is not the same thing as the people involved. You're burning the bridge because the bridge is not conducive to your principles and doesn't move you forward. But when you burn a bridge, you're not burning the person, so to speak. You're burning a path that has led to a situation that isn't good for your life. You don't have to hate any of the people involved or think that they are bad people. But what they're bringing into your life is simply not good for you. (We'll talk more about this later when we discuss forgiveness.)

Some Questions for You to Address

Burning bridges is a big piece of the process we're working on together. You can't become the greatest you as long as you have bridges leading you to places that keep you from growing. Burning bridges requires facing some tough realities

90

about your situation and your vision of your future, so I'd like you to answer a few more questions before we move on:

- Where are all of the bridges in your life leading you?
- Can you tell the difference between a bridge that needs burning and one that just needs some repairs?
- Who is draining you?
- How much does your future matter to you?
- Which future looks better: the one where you stay in your current situation or the one where you go?

We've got some more challenging work to do in the next chapter, but you're up for it by now, I'm sure. Just getting where you are in the process already means that you have the stuff you need to keep going.

5

DIGGING UP THE BAD SEEDS

I'm betting a lot of you can relate to this story: When I was in second grade, my teacher looked me right in the eye and told me that she was sure I wasn't going to amount to anything. She didn't say it *exactly* that way, but she was highly critical of me and dismissive of anything that interested me, and what I *heard* was that she thought I was going nowhere. Did I mention that I was in second grade at the time?

This made a pretty big impression on me. My teacher was an authority figure, and I'd been taught to respect authority figures, so I just assumed that she knew more about me than I knew about myself. So if she thought I wasn't destined to do anything special, maybe she was right. Her opinion certainly stuck with me. Whenever I hit a roadblock in my life, I would think about that teacher and imagine her nodding and saying, "I knew he was headed for no good."

When I started playing football, a similar thing happened with a coach. I was a star player from the time I was little, but this guy wasn't buying it. He told me I wasn't good enough to make it in football, and he reminded me of his opinion every chance he got. Here was another key figure in my life who thought I wasn't going to be able to reach my goals, and again, this opinion stuck with me. Whenever I struggled on the field, I would hear this coach's voice in my head and think that he knew what he was talking about, even when lots of other people felt very differently and my stats suggested otherwise.

Not that long ago, I ran into an old acquaintance, and we started talking. He said to me, "Are you still doing that little RehabTime thing?" That's the only thing I remember from that conversation, because once he said that, I didn't hear anything else. And even though my videos were being watched by millions of people by that point, I still walked away thinking, *Is RehabTime just a little thing?*

All of these people interacted with me in such a way that they planted seeds within me. Seeds of doubt. Seeds of negativity. And these seeds took root and had an impact on my opinion about myself. They were like the crabgrass choking off the beautiful flowers in the garden of my ambitions and my dreams. And just like crabgrass, it wasn't easy to get rid of these things; I'd chop them down and they'd just keep growing back. And that kept on happening until I found myself some very powerful weed killer.

It took me a long time to figure out what was going on

here. It wasn't until I started speaking to large groups of people and talking to them about their own histories that I realized we all have gardens filled with fantastic plants and flowers, but they are under attack all the time from the weeds that were planted there by people who may or may not have known what they were doing and may or may not have intended us harm. And until we get those weeds out of our gardens, we're never going to grow the way we should and the way we deserve to.

These weeds are the result of what I call "bad seeds." And here's the thing about bad seeds: they grow really easily and really fast, and they're extremely hard to eliminate. It takes some special gardening tools to get rid of them. Fortunately, I've got the tools for you in this chapter.

What Bad Seeds Are

There are many different kinds of bad seeds out there. There are those seeds that make us think we can't do what we really want to do. Those were the kind planted by my childhood football coach. Maybe you have a big ambition for your life. You want to start a business, achieve success locally, and then open that business all over the country or even all over the world. But while you're still in the planning stage, someone reads you a bunch of statistics about how most new businesses fail and the odds of doing okay even at a local level are stacked against you. Or maybe you've been a stay-at-home mom for years, but now your kids can take care of themselves to the point where you can go back to school and finish your education. When you mention this to a friend, he or she reacts by saying how hard it is to go back to school at your age and how your family responsibilities are going to make it really tough to get the grades you need to get a degree.

Sometimes bad seeds sprout up as doubts that you've been trying to overcome. You think you're ready to become a manager at your company, but you've never actually had a management position, so you're not absolutely certain. Then someone plants a bad seed by reminding you of a time when you struggled at work, and that chokes off your confidence and makes you question whether you are management material. Maybe instead you're thinking about moving to a new town and starting a new life on your own, but you're worried about doing this because you've always had a big support group around you and you won't have one in this new town. One day, you mention your plans to an acquaintance, and that person says, "You want to move to another city? You'll be running back here within six months." This reinforces all of your concerns about the move and suddenly makes you feel that you're out of your mind for even considering doing something like that.

Many of the worst seeds come from our histories. Our families especially can plant a lot of bad seeds in us because we're so vulnerable to their opinions and approval. If a parent spends a lot of time telling you how much you've disappointed him or her, those seeds are going to leave very deep roots. If you don't deal with this, you could spend your entire life thinking that you're going to let down everyone around you to the point where you don't even try to do more than the minimum. If your sister berated you about your social skills from an early age, you might be convinced you're terrible at talking to people or making friends, and this might cause you to avoid trying to connect with others. If the person saying this was a classmate instead of your sister, you might have blown it off or at least not taken it as seriously. But because it's your sister—someone you look up to and who you think knows you well—this statement becomes part of how you define yourself.

Then there's the history of our circumstances. The situations we grow up in are especially influential in how we see the world later in life. Maybe your parents had a really toxic relationship. They were always cutting each other down and sucking all the love out of the household. A situation like that is a dangerous seed because it could give you the impression that this is how all households are and either lead you to avoid creating your own household when you're an adult or make you repeat these negative behaviors in your own household. We've all heard about the cycle of repeating dysfunctional and abusive behaviors from one generation to the next. That's because the bad seeds grow and take over and they are especially hard to dig out.

Then, of course, there is our relational history. Relationships can plant some of the toughest seeds to dig up, especially early relationships, because you don't have anything to compare them to. If your first best friend winds up embarrassing you in front of a group of people before dumping you to be with that group, you're likely to be much more cautious about making close friendships in the future. If you fall head-over-heels in love with a guy and then he cheats on you or dumps you so he can play the field, that's going to be in the back of your mind any time another guy tries to get close. It may even cause you to hurt that other person before he gets the chance to hurt you, starting a pattern where you blow up your romances before they can ever get serious.

Rehabber Jelica told me the story of a bad-seed relationship that absolutely needed to be dug up. After seventeen years of marriage to a man she truly loved, she'd gotten divorced because he'd cheated on her. While she was still feeling heartbroken over this, she began dating someone else who made her feel special—for a short while. Then things started to go south. Whenever they were out together, he'd insist that she look at the floor because he didn't want her making eye contact with anyone. He began to accuse her of being unfaithful, even though she did everything she could to prove that she wasn't. He prevented her from spending time with her family and friends and even dropped her off at work so he knew where she was at all times. Things got so rough that Jelica felt like she was in a bad Lifetime movie.

Meanwhile, the bad seed this guy had planted in Jelica's life was putting down roots in other people's lives too. Her children begged her to leave this man, because he'd even become threatening to their father.

Jelica was able to get away long enough to take her kids for a visit to her parents' house in Florida. While she was there, she finally had the opportunity to face up to the situation she'd been dealing with.

"I prayed real hard. I asked God to help me to get out because I didn't know how. I had my house and a good job back at home, and I knew he [the man] would never leave me alone. But after a long talk with God . . . BOOM."

When Jelica saw clearly that she needed to dig this bad seed out of her life, everything started falling into place.

"All these doors started opening. My parents offered to let me stay there until I found a place. I got a job offer after applying to a few places. A close friend of mine called me, seeking a place to live, so I was able to rent my house to her. And the father of my kids actually wanted me to leave and was willing to sacrifice and travel to see the kids because he wanted us safe.

"I was able to sell 90 percent of my things. A couple even gave me extra for some of my furniture. They said, 'I don't know what you're going through, but please accept the overpayment,' and they wished me blessings."

Digging up this bad seed was a painful experience for Jelica, but it has left her in a much better place.

"I have finally stopped looking around when I leave my house or work. I've stopped feeling nervous about private calls. And most importantly, I finally have more peaceful days than ones with anxiety and depression. I made a commitment to do everything that I always wanted and not ever put up with crap from a man again. I strive every day to love myself. And I'm learning to do just that. My kids are so happy."

Jelica's story hits hard on the biggest problem with bad seeds, which is that they prevent us from being the best version of ourselves. They do this in three ways: they make us timid, they make us doubt, and they make us mistrust. It's almost impossible to get where you want to go if these three conditions have a big place in your life. If you're timid, you're not going to put yourself out there and go after the opportunities that could take you to someplace great. If you have doubt, you might decide that your ambitions are nothing but crazy fantasies, and you'll wind up settling for much less than what you're capable of having. And if you mistrust, you won't open your heart to people who actually deserve your trust. One of the things I always say to people is that they can't let the heart that didn't love them keep them from the hearts that will. Yes, it's important to protect yourself from hurt, but if your history causes you to protect yourself so much that you never let anyone in, then that history has done far too much damage. You will need to deal with that.

While a lot of the seeds that get planted in us are planted when we are young, they are definitely not the only ones. In fact, new seeds are planted in you just about every day. You could see something on television that has an effect on your confidence, your body image, your sense of how the world works. You could run into a friend on the street who asks you a question that makes you wonder how people perceive you and what they say about you when you're not around. You might go to a family dinner and have lots of old behaviors play out across the table, planting new seeds in the process. You could go on social media, read a post that has absolutely nothing to do with you, and still feel like you read a commentary on your life.

Seeds are everywhere. Not all of them are going to take root, of course. Just like the acorns that fall from trees, few of them will actually grow into anything that really matters. But it's important to understand that seeds are all around you and that the bad ones can do some real damage if you're not paying attention to them and digging them up as soon as you find them.

And while we're talking about this, let's talk for a minute

about other people's opinions. Let's get real about something right now: other people's opinions don't matter. A lot of people miss this. I know. I had to learn this for myself. When I first started speaking, people told me that I didn't have the gifts to be a speaker. They said that speaking wasn't for me, and that maybe I should try something different. Those opinions planted seeds of doubt in me, and I had to dig them up, because if I had listened to those opinions, I wouldn't be where I am now.

And you know what? The people who were saying these things to me had no qualifications for saying them. This kind of thing happens all the time, and you have to watch out for it. A lot of times we take opinions from people who have never been where we're trying to go or have maybe even failed at what we're trying to do. But you should never take an opinion from someone who hasn't had success with whatever you're trying to do. Never let other people plant their impossibilities in your life. What they couldn't do has nothing to do with what you can do. What they can't be has nothing to do with what you can be. A lot of people take their bad experiences and put those experiences on someone else. They'll choke off your garden with the bad seeds of their opinions. Don't let that happen to you.

The Good Seeds

Before I get to how to dig up your bad seeds, I want to point out that there are plenty of good seeds out there, and you definitely want to keep those planted and growing in your garden. So, what is a good seed, and how can you tell the difference between a good one and a bad one? Good seeds are anything that helps you grow and flower.

Something I didn't know during the gardening adventure I told you about in the last chapter but that I know now is that the pros will put plants together that benefit one another. For example, one plant might keep pests away from another plant, or one might help make the soil better for another plant. When these "seeds" work in tandem, the whole garden is better for it.

Good seeds are kind of like that for you, and in lots of ways they're the exact opposite of bad seeds. If a bad seed is someone who reminds you of a time you had trouble with or failed at something, a good seed is someone who reminds you that you've overcome troubles in the past. If a bad seed is a family member who keeps putting you down or limiting your potential, a good seed is a family member who supports your dreams and encourages you to make the most of yourself. If a bad seed is a seriously dysfunctional relationship between your parents, a good seed is seeing your parents be affectionate with one another and be on the same team.

For Rehabber Jeannine, a good seed was sown in her life at a time when she desperately needed it. For ten years, she dated a man she describes as "toxic." Jeannine's son hated the man, but Jeannine refused to leave him, because she'd convinced herself that she couldn't do any better. Even when this man and her son got into a "knock-down, drag-out fight," Jeannine still wouldn't dump the guy. Her parents, from whom she rented her home, demanded that she kick the guy out, and when Jeannine refused, they evicted her.

"I lost everything," she told me. "Everything! My home, my job, my son. I was homeless. I had nothing. I ended up in a tent. Alone. Scared."

She made some new friends who let her stay with them at a local motel, but when she discovered that they were using heroin, she realized she had to get out of there—but that meant being homeless once again. Desperate, she called a girlfriend, Nancy, who said Jeannine could stay with her. Nancy had actually offered Jeannine help before, but Jeannine turned her down because she didn't have anything she could offer in return.

"Nancy always gave me 'props.' She knew that I was having a difficult time with self-worth. So she made me feel as though I was important. Little things, such as helping her with her kids, as my son was not with me at the time, helped. She taught me how to cook new dishes. She gave me attention that I had been lacking for so long. I was always the one to hop up and help people—with money, time, gas, whatever. She didn't give me material things, but she did give me some of my self-esteem back. She made me realize true friends don't ask for things. They just want to spend time with you. Encourage you. Cheer you on. She helped me when no one else would. She loved me unconditionally. While I was with her, I got back on my feet. I got a job. I got a room to rent. And I saw my son for the first time in months. And she never asked me for anything! Not anything.

"Good seeds boost you up. Bad ones tear you down. And I'm no longer being torn because she showed me what true friendship was."

This isn't to say that good seeds always feel good when

they're planted. Some of the best seeds you can get come in the form of constructive criticism. Now, I don't know about you, but I'm not always thrilled to get criticism of any kind. Sometimes, I just want people to tell me that what I'm doing is great, especially if *I* think it's great. But when someone points out a flaw in something you're doing, and he or she does it with love and respect and without making any effort to tear you down, that person is planting a good seed in your life that is important for you to cultivate. It will not only sprout up and beautify your garden, but if it's the right kind of criticism, it can make your garden better forever. The moment it's planted, it might not feel so good, but you know it's going to help you grow.

This raises a question: If bad seeds can sometimes feel good and good seeds can sometimes feel bad, how can you tell the difference? This involves a certain amount of knowing yourself and a certain ability to predict the future. Let's look at a good seed that might feel less than good at the start. You're making a presentation at work and you think you are doing a fantastic job. People seem to be paying attention, and they ask good questions when you are finished. Afterward, though, your boss comes by and says that you did good work overall, but if you'd done a few things differently, the presentation would have been way better. Your first reaction is to think that your boss is bringing you down. You're sure you nailed that presentation, and she's just trying to put you in your place because she's jealous of you. Maybe you even think you'll need to find another job if you want to get ahead, because your boss is planting all kinds of bad seeds.

But step back from that for a second. First, didn't your

boss begin with the positive, saying you did a good job? If all she wanted to do was tear you down, why would she say that? Next, look at yourself. Maybe if you're being really honest, you'll admit that you tend not to do your absolute best when pretty good will do. If that's the case, isn't your boss just showing you the difference between the two? Okay. Now do a little predicting of the future. If you stick with pretty good, you'll probably keep your job and might even get a promotion at some point. But if you do your absolute best, you could perhaps be running the whole department—or even something better. Would you get that far if your boss wasn't coaching you up? So, in thinking about it, that seed that might have appeared to be bad when it first went in the ground was actually a really good one, because it is definitely making your garden better.

Now, let's look at a bad seed that might not seem so bad at first. You're out with a bunch of people you go out with pretty regularly. One of these people encourages you to be less inhibited when you're out in public, telling you that you'd have more fun if you were a little wilder and a little more provocative. You try this out, and it certainly seems like great advice. More people are paying attention to you, more guys are approaching you, and you're definitely having a better time than you'd been having recently.

But what do you know about yourself? Are you comfortable being the life of the party? When you go home, do you feel like you've had the time of your life, or are you a little embarrassed about what you might have done and the impression you might have made? Jump forward a month or six months or a year. Is this behavior going to feel good then, or is it going to turn you into someone you don't really want to be and surround you with people you don't really want to be with? If that's the case, your friend planted a bad seed. Maybe she didn't realize she was doing this—lots of times people who plant bad seeds don't intend to hurt you—but if she's trying to turn you into someone you're not or someone you don't want to be, she's not helping you grow and could in fact be killing your garden.

So, when you're trying to distinguish between the good seeds and the bad seeds in your life, you need to think about all of this. Ask yourself what this seed's growth is doing to your garden—not just today, but most important, in the future. If it's helping your garden grow, then keep it. But if it's choking off your garden—dig it up.

Digging Up the Bad Seeds

Digging up bad seeds involves three key steps. The first step is to use the tool we developed in the last chapter and get some of the bad influences out of your life. The thing about bad seeds is that you can't just chop them off when they start to sprout. The sprout is just the top of the seed. What really matters is the root, and if a bad seed has taken root, it's going to keep growing no matter what you do at the surface level. For example, if someone is regularly making you feel awful about yourself, it isn't enough to take a break from being with that individual. If he or she is truly planting bad seeds in your life, you need to separate from that person completely. Otherwise, you might feel a little better for a short while by cutting off the sprout and taking a break from that relationship, but the root is still there, and the next time you see that person, it's going to sprout up again and keep sprouting until you do something more permanent.

We've already talked about the pain and difficulty associated with cutting someone out of your life, but I think it bears repeating: while the temporary pain might be bad, it is much, much better than the ongoing pain you're going to keep feeling if you don't make a clean break from that individual.

As important as this step is, there's another that's even more important: prioritizing facts over feelings. This is not the simplest of processes, but it's critical. Look, I get it. I know how easy it is to let my feelings influence me, so I'm definitely not blaming you if you do the same thing. Someone says something that hurts me, and I let it work its way inside of me. When my coach told me I was never going to be a success as a football player, I let that get into my head. After practices, I would tell myself that maybe I was never going to be good enough. If I made a mistake on the field, I would see that as confirmation that Coach was right and that I was just kidding myself about the whole football thing.

Bad seeds mess with your head. They hurt your confidence, or they cast a shadow over your self-image, or they keep you from reaching for your goals because you don't believe you can attain those goals. The reason bad seeds are so bad is that they're actually effective at doing you harm. If you're driving and some random person honks at you because you didn't make a left turn fast enough, that's not a bad seed. That honk was just someone being impatient, and you understand that. But if a friend tells you that you drive like you're scared all the time, that's going to affect you in an entirely different way. You might even start to wonder if you're a bad driver and become self-conscious every time you get behind the wheel.

That's when it's time to separate facts from feelings. If you were a bad driver, you'd be getting into lots of accidents or at least you'd be having a lot of close calls. But you haven't had a single accident, and you can't even remember the last time you had a near miss. Yeah, you might be a little cautious when you're out on the road, but that's worked out pretty well for you and everyone else, because you're staying safe and you're not endangering anyone around you.

Remember that guy I told you about who asked me if I was still doing my "little RehabTime thing"? As I've already admitted, that got to me for a moment. I allowed myself to wonder if maybe RehabTime wasn't having the impact I thought it was. Otherwise, this guy would have known all about it, right? That lasted no more than a few minutes, though. Then I looked at the facts—at all the people I know I've touched with RehabTime, at the numbers of people who'd watched my videos and interacted with me and reached out to let me know how I'd inspired them. And because I prioritized the facts over my feelings, I didn't let that bad seed take root. I just tossed it out of my garden and went on doing what I could to help people with RehabTime.

So, what I want you to do with all of your bad seeds is respect your feelings, but let the facts take charge. Someone tells you that you don't have the emotional strength to make it on your own in a new city? Well, the facts suggest that every time you've gone into a brand-new situation, you've gotten comfortable in that situation within a few months, so dig that bad seed out of the ground, because you're going to do great when you move. Your father tells you that you've always been a disappointment to him? Well, you've got a good job, good friends, and a history of overcoming setbacks. Does that sound like a disappointment? That bad seed probably has really deep roots, but get in there and dig it all the way out, because the facts don't lie: you're anything but a disappointment. You've gone through a series of bad relationships, and you're starting to believe you can never have a good one? Well, maybe that's because your parents had an awful relationship and that's the model you're used to, but now that you realize how much damage that bad seed has caused, you're ready to see that you're a lovable, caring person who just needs to take a different approach to relationships. Toss that bad seed out of your garden.

Let's be real about something right now: you're reading this book, you're actively trying to become the best version of you, we've already put in a ton of work together, and you're ready to put in a ton more. If that's the case, then the facts are going to be on your side *most of the time*. You're the kind of person who wants better things for yourself and the people you love. That means that when you get beneath the surface to where the bad seeds are taking root, you're going to be able to dig up these seeds with facts—the facts that show that you are fundamentally better than your detractors would have you believe.

The third step for digging up the bad seeds is something we're going to spend the entire next chapter on, so I'm just going to touch on it here: forgiveness. It's impossible to dig up your bad seeds without forgiveness, because until you forgive, you're going to keep carrying that seed around with you, and it's going to wind up getting planted again. Maybe you've removed that person from your life. Maybe you've convinced yourself that whatever that person had been telling you, the facts tell a different story. But now you have to forgive, even if forgiveness seems just about impossible. The seeds won't be truly gone until you do.

Circling Back

Before we get to forgiveness, I want to make sure you have a good idea about what bad seeds are and how to deal with them. Take as much time as you need now to think about these questions:

- What is creating doubt inside of you?
- What is it about your history that is making it hard for you to grow?
- What is it about your current circumstances that is making it hard for you to grow?
- Who is planting good seeds in your life?
- Are you ready to separate the facts from your feelings and let the facts rule the day?

Now that we've covered this, you're ready to learn more about the power of forgiveness and who benefits most when you forgive.

6

FORGIVENESS IS
NOT FOR OTHERS—
IT'S FOR YOU

G atholo has not had an easy life. Nobody was really there for her, and when she was growing up, kids in school teased her mercilessly, calling her "the girl with the big forehead." She was bullied constantly, and things got even worse for her when she got her period before the rest of her classmates.

"They somehow found out and made fun of me," she told me. "It was so embarrassing! I hated myself for developing earlier than my peers."

She hoped that when she moved to high school, things would be different, but that turned out not to be the case.

"I felt neglected, unloved, and always had to try so hard to fit in. My first boyfriend tried being there for me, but at some point, he cheated. For me the relationship was serious because I've always wanted someone permanent in my life to actually love me. I had to change schools in grade eleven, and that's when I lost my best friend. Though it was a relief of some sort because she was so judgmental and always wanted things done her way, I was really hurt when we couldn't be friends anymore, because I really loved her.

"I tried making new friends at the new school, and it seemed to be working at first, until they also started commenting on how I look. When all my relationships weren't working out, the worst just happened. I almost got raped in my house by a person who was like a brother to me. And when I told my family about it, they didn't want to do anything about it. Everything that was happening just proved to me that nobody really cared."

Now twenty, Gatholo has made some important adjustments in her life that have helped her, but she still feels deeply scarred by all of the awful and hurtful things people have done to her—and she's carrying that around with her.

"I know at some point I'm going to have to forgive and completely let go. The truth is, forgiving someone who is not sorry is hard. All these people don't know the damage they've caused. It still hurts thinking about what they've done and how they are all carrying on with life while I have to deal with all these demons. I'd be lying if I said I had forgiven them. I want to, but I don't know how to go about it."

Letting Go Isn't Easy

While Gatholo has faced more challenges in her life than many of us, we all have some version of her story in our lives. We all have someone who has done us so much wrong that we just can't let go of the anger and resentment we feel. Hey, I've probably made your list of such people even longer with this book and its encouragement to look deep into your life and burn bridges and dig up bad seeds. Sorry about that. But you know why I did it, and it's really important that I did. Identifying this stuff, however, is very different from moving on from it—and moving on can be a real challenge, even though it's critical that you do.

If you're like most people, you hold on to this stuff for a simple reason: because it's hard to let it go. This person or this group of people really hurt you. They didn't just do something that made you angry; they did something that affected your life in a major way. Maybe it was a good friend gone bad. Maybe it was someone who took something from you. Maybe it was a person who actively tried to hurt your reputation or your standing in your community. When you're faced with something like this, you might move on from it physically—you end the friendship, you make sure that person can't take anything else from you, and you block that person out of your life—but it's a lot harder to move on from it emotionally. And until you've moved on from it emotionally, you haven't moved on at all. What you need to do is forgive. Without forgiveness, you can *move away* from the pain, but you'll never *move on* from the pain.

But forgiveness can be tough. Yet, it's also 100 percent

necessary. You're not going to be able to take big steps forward with your life and become the best version of yourself if you're carrying around a huge amount of anger and resentment and holding grudges over past hurts. As long as you hold on to anger, you're letting someone who is no longer a part of your life control the life you're living now. That's the effect that harboring anger and resentment has on you, and it is very damaging. This can play out in any number of ways. Someone betrays your trust, so you become a less trusting person, no longer allowing yourself to get close to people. As a result, you have fewer people in your inner circle. So do the math: because one person betrayed your trust at some point in your life, you've taken steps that have made your life smaller.

Or maybe you were in a romantic relationship with someone who left you in an awful way, and because of this, you're wary of committing yourself to any other relationship because you never want to feel that level of pain again. This is just another version of the previous scenario: someone who did a bad thing to you earlier in your life is *continuing* to do that bad thing to you. He or she affected the way you conduct your life, altering your ability to open yourself to someone who might love you the way you deserve to be loved.

Or, maybe a parent was too damaged or too caught up in his or her own stuff to give you the nurturing you needed. Instead your mom or dad made you feel unwanted. As a result, you avoid having children because you're worried that the model this person set for you is the model you're going to use as a parent, and you don't want to inflict that on an innocent kid. In this case, this unforgiven parent continues to have such an effect on your life that it's literally threatening future generations.

I could go on and on with examples, but I think the point is clear: as long as you harbor anger and resentment, as long as you keep carrying grudges, the people who did you wrong will keep doing you wrong. It's as if they're still right there next to you, causing you all kinds of hurt. You've got to forgive these people in order to move on, and the sooner you do this, the better. When we don't forgive, we make other people pay for mistakes they didn't make.

But forgiveness is hard, right? I'm not denying that, but we're going to work on this right now so it gets easier for you.

Let's start here: I think that the reason most of us find it so tough to forgive is that we think forgiveness is a gift you give to someone else. You've been wronged by somebody, so why would you want to give him a gift? But that's not really the case at all. Forgiveness is a gift you give yourself, because when you forgive, you free yourself from the control of others who don't mean the best for you. Forgiveness is taking your power back. They controlled your past; don't give them the power to control your future. It's understandable that you might think that forgiveness is a way of letting the other person win. But exactly the opposite is true. When you forgive, you finally triumph over the thing that he or she did to you. You finally let it stop controlling your life. Lots of people think of forgiveness as a sign of weakness, but it is most definitely not that. In fact, it's one of the strongest things you can do because it is an act of liberation. It's a tool that's going to improve your whole life.

Thinking About the People
Who Have Hurt You

We are all imperfect. We're filled with flaws, some little and some big, and these flaws are a large part of what makes us human. But these imperfections lead us to do things to each other that we shouldn't do, even when we know we're doing the other person harm.

Hurt people hurt people. I'm sure you've heard this phrase before, but how much have you really thought about it? When people have had bad things done to them over the course of their lives, they tend to respond by doing bad things to other people. They become the pain that someone else inflicted upon them, the pain that they hated. That's one of the key reasons why forgiveness is so important—it's essential to break out of this cycle. Letting the hurt go allows you to move beyond the hurt, and we're going to talk more about that momentarily. For now, though, I want you to spend some more time thinking about the people who have hurt you.

There's an excellent chance that every one of these people has suffered some serious damage of their own. Maybe they were abused or bullied. Maybe they let the wrongs in their lives fester inside of them. Maybe they were neglected or filled up with hate by people who were supposed to nurture them. Because they have these things in their past and they probably haven't done their own forgiving, they impose the damage they've suffered on others. And you happened to wind up in their sights.

That doesn't in any way make what they've done to you right. But it does make it a little bit easier for you to understand and maybe even relate to. In fact, there's a pretty good chance that you've even been on the other side of this yourself. Go back to the times you've hurt someone else, even if it's painful to think about. Can you trace the pain you inflicted back to a hurt you'd previously received? If so, it might help you to understand how you got hurt in the first place.

Again, I'm not making excuses for what was done to you. I'm just giving you some important context. Empathy is a precious tool, and it's one that you want to use as often as you can, not just here but everywhere in your life. Put yourself in the other person's shoes and understand that he was probably carrying a legacy of hurt forward, and if he had only understood how important it was to forgive, maybe the chain would have ended before it ever got to you. Once you see it that way, you can begin the process of moving on from the hurt you received because you can begin to see it as something other than pure malice.

And while we're looking at this hurt from the other person's perspective, here's something else to keep in mind: there's a really good chance that the other person knows exactly what she did to you. Sure, there are some people who are so used to treating people badly that they might not even remember doing something bad to you specifically. For the most part, though, when something bad goes down between two people, both of you know what happened. And there's a good chance that both of you were affected by it in some way. That's another reality about the way people touch each other's lives for good and bad. When you've hurt somebody, you know, right? Yeah, it's possible that somebody out there is feeling a lot of pain over something that you don't even realize you did to that person, but for the most part you know. There's even a good chance that you feel bad about doing it. Certainly, I feel bad about the times when I've really hurt someone. Remember the woman I cheated on from chapter 1? I feel terrible that I handled things that way, and I feel especially terrible about how it affected my mother and that woman's mother, who previously had been best friends. So, when you think about the people you need to forgive, consider the fact that while you're harboring anger and resentment over this grudge, there's a really good chance that the person who did it to you is harboring regrets.

But I'm only saying this to make you more sensitive to the need for empathy. Right now, this isn't about the other person; it's about you. And granting forgiveness is one of the best and most powerful things you can do for yourself.

Rehabber Betha got some help getting to this point, and it made a huge difference for her. "Growing up, I didn't have an easy life," she told me. "I was scared all the time and I never felt loved."

Her parents divorced when she was four, and her stepfather sexually abused her for eight years. She eventually moved in with her father, but he died a couple of years later, leaving Betha with a stepmother with a violent temper. When her brother contacted the Department of Social Services, things got even worse.

"The man from DSS went to my house, but no one was home. He left a message on our answering machine that revealed too many details about our situation. My stepmother heard it and called when I got home. She informed me that she was on the way home and that both of us would die when she got there." Betha's stepmother didn't end up making good on her threats, but you see the situation Betha was in.

Not long after that, Betha started dating a man, ended up pregnant, and married him. But this man turned out to be abusive. He pushed her down a flight of stairs, causing her to lose the baby, after which he became increasingly more abusive and controlling.

These were just some of the people who had done her wrong, so Betha was understandably carrying around all kinds of resentment. That was when a conversation made a big change in her life.

"I had been through eight years of molestation and physical and verbal abuse—and not being protected from any of it by my mother, who knew about it and did nothing to stop it—of being raped twice by two different men I trusted, and of having almost $40,000 stolen from me. This left me with a lot of bitterness and anger. These events played through my head every single day. I carried them with me. I guarded myself against everyone and wouldn't let anyone (family or friend) in to see the real me. I pushed everyone away. I was angry. I was bitter. I was hateful. I was even cruel when there was no need for that.

"Then I had a conversation with a person who asked me how long I was going to carry it around with me. They explained that every day I woke up with it on my mind and ruling my behavior and thoughts, it was like drinking poison and expecting it to kill the other person. The person also explained to me that I had to find a way to forgive those people and put it past me or it would destroy me, my life, and any chance of finding happiness in my future.

"Then the last thing that was said was this: 'Go stand in front of a mirror for fifteen minutes and look at the person looking back at you. Make mental notes of what you see. Not of what your features look like but of the attitude you present when someone looks at you. If you like that person, ignore what we have talked about. If you don't, then figure out whatever you have to do to forgive [your offenders] and move forward. It's not easy, but if you survived it, you can heal from it. But the first step is forgiveness.'

"So, I did. I went and looked in the mirror and I remember crying. I didn't like the person that was staring back at me. I asked God to help me to forgive [my offenders]. I started by praying for them. And my first prayer was 'God be with them.' Later, that changed to more personal prayers. I didn't stop there though, because most of my situations had been situations where I had felt violated or like I had lost my power over myself. I learned self-defense. I connected with other survivors of rape. I joined a speakers group, where I have written about and spoken about my experiences and what I've been through. I started a blog. I went to therapy to learn coping techniques, and then I share what I learned with everyone I meet who might need help. I found that the more I prayed and the more I did to reclaim my power, educate others, and stand alongside those who were going through situations that I had been through, the more my forgiveness came.

"I think my biggest hang-up for a while was that I thought if I forgave [my offenders] it was like saying that what they had done was okay or that it had never happened. But I had to come to the realization that it wasn't the case. It wasn't okay. It did happen. And me saying, 'I forgive you'—whether actually to them or just inside to let go of it—was a way of acknowledging that, yes, you hurt me and, no, it wasn't right, but you will not destroy me by what you did—I'm reclaiming what you took from me."

The Power You Get from Forgiveness

Forgiveness is a huge act of *giving*—you are offering the end of your anger and resentment to someone who has done you wrong. But it is also a huge act of *getting*, and that's what I want to concentrate on here. When you forgive, you get an enormous amount of power in return. This power comes in a number of forms. First, there's the power that comes from being freed from emotional burdens. If you've ever worked out while wearing weights, you know that when you take those weights off, you feel like you can move twice as fast as you did before. Forgiveness has the same kind of effect on your spirit. The long-term anger you feel toward someone else puts a huge burden on your back. You carry that around all the time. Even when you're not feeling angry, it's still there in the back of your mind because you haven't fully processed the hurt you received. How much better would it feel to throw off all of that extra weight you've been carrying?

When you forgive, you feel emotionally lighter, and that lightness gives you the power to do way more productive stuff with your life. It really is like taking off those weights after a strenuous workout; just as you feel like you can run twice as fast with the weights off, you'll feel you can reach twice as many goals when you get rid of the old grudges you've been carrying.

The next power you get is the power that comes when you soften your heart. When you're convinced that you can't forgive someone, your heart gets a little harder all the time. That hardness accumulates, and it can make a mess of your other relationships. Maybe you had a really bad breakup years ago and you finally met someone else and got married, but you're not giving your wife everything she needs emotionally because you're still protecting yourself from a past hurt that you haven't forgiven. Maybe you've made some new friends recently, but you're not really offering your friendship the way you once did with earlier friends because your heart was hardened by a friendship that went sour and you haven't been able to let that go. If you can remember back to a time when you didn't feel so guarded and protective of your emotions, you can probably remember how great it felt to connect with the people who mattered the most to you in an unburdened way. Your heart was softer then, and that softness allowed you to enjoy things that you stop enjoying when your heart hardens. That's a power you can have back when you choose to forgive, move on from your biggest hurts, and give the important people in your life everything they deserve to receive from you.

Maybe the most important power that comes with forgiveness is the power to live your own life. I can't emphasize enough how much control you give to other people when you allow the way they hurt you to keep hurting you. In little ways (and sometimes in not-so-little ways), if you hold on to feelings of anger and resentment over someone who did you wrong, you're letting that person control a piece of your life. You aren't in charge of some of your actions and many of your emotions because someone else, by what he or she did to you in the past, is dictating them from a distance. That's a crazy amount of power to give to someone else—especially someone who has proven that he or she doesn't have your best interests at heart. And this gets worse and worse if you have multiple grudges in your life that you need to forgive. At some point, these grudges take over, with the result that other people are manipulating most of your actions. Forgiveness takes that control and that power back. Forgiveness takes your *life* back. Once you forgive what someone did to you, the power over how you deal with the legacy of that person's offense returns to you. He or she no longer gets a say in how you conduct your life moving forward. That's all yours, which is exactly the way it should be.

I felt this power in a big way when I finally decided to forgive football. As you know, by the end of my time trying to make it in the NFL, I was feeling pretty bitter about the whole thing and I wasn't in a good place at all. I did a lot of hard work on myself and got my life moving in the right direction, and things were going really well for me. I had a wife and kid I loved; I had work that inspired me; I had new friends. But even after I was living the life I wanted to live in so many ways, I was still carrying around a ton of resentment over the way things had turned out for me in professional football. This had such an effect that I couldn't watch football at all, and I had a very tough time watching *any* sports—this from a guy who always loved sports and defined himself by football for a big part of his life.

I don't think I fully realized the effect this was having on me until my son got old enough to participate in sports, and I decided that I didn't want him going out for any teams. This was really tough for him, because Tristan has turned out to be a natural athlete, and he was dying to get out on the field. But my bitterness about what football had done to me was still so strong that I was letting that experience control me in one of my most important roles—as Tristan's father. I made a lot of excuses, mostly to convince myself and others that I was taking this position to prevent Tristan from injury. But when I finally realized that this was all because I never got over what happened to me in the NFL, I knew I had to deal with it. I couldn't let something from my past affect my son's future. And dealing with it started with forgiving the NFL for not giving me the chance I thought I deserved. I had to put it completely behind me and even accept the fact that missing out on professional football led me down a great path that I might never have gone down if I'd made an NFL roster.

Once that happened, once I could finally say, "Okay, it's over," I got a real power boost, because my feelings about the NFL were no longer weighing me down. I could watch and enjoy sports again and, most important, I could allow Tristan to fall in love with sports and truly appreciate how much he was enjoying it.

They're Not Getting Away with Anything

One of the biggest problems people have with forgiveness is the feeling that if you forgive, you're letting the other person get away with what he or she did to you. If you feel that way, I completely understand. You wouldn't be carrying this pain around with you for all of this time if what was done to you wasn't bad. Someone hurt you badly, and you don't want to say that it was okay for that person to hurt you.

The truth is, if we're really being honest, the person has probably already gotten away with it. She's moved on with her life and likely doesn't spend much time (if any) thinking about what happened between the two of you. She's out there living her life and maybe doing the same thing she did to you to someone else. This is a really important point. If you're hung up about someone getting away with doing something bad to you, how is your being hung up about it *preventing* that person from getting away with it? All it's really doing is deepening the effect she's already had on you, which means that she's still getting away with stuff.

Of course, there's also a really good chance that she didn't actually get away with it. Not really. As I mentioned earlier, when someone hurts someone else, that person usually knows what she did. Maybe she has a really guilty conscience about it, and she beats herself up about it regularly. Maybe she has a history of treating people this way and it has finally caught up to her and people are starting to steer clear of her. Maybe it's karma or God's will or whatever, but maybe she's actually paid for what she did to you, several times. Whether she has or not, holding on to your feelings of anger or resentment isn't going to change how this resolves in her life. She's going to have to deal with what she did to you at some point—hey, she might even become a better person when she realizes what she did wrong—but your forgiving her means that you can stop dealing with it and go on to way more productive things.

I also think it's important to explain what forgiveness

doesn't mean for you. We're going to get into the steps involved shortly, but before we do, let me say what forgiveness is not. Forgiveness does not require you to share that forgiveness with the other person. Maybe you feel that you can't forgive because you can't get yourself to see that guy again or text him to get the conversation started. Don't let that stop you. You are absolutely not required to let someone know you've forgiven him in order to benefit from the power that comes from forgiveness. Forgiveness is all about making peace with a troublesome episode in your life, and it's an entirely personal thing. If you've already deleted that guy from your phone, there's no need to try to find his number. You don't need to get in touch with any of his friends or look him up on social media. Instead, delete him from the rest of your life and, most important, from your mind. Forgiveness doesn't always need "proper" closure. I see so many people delay their healing because they're trying to find closure. Waiting for the apology, waiting for the understanding. Sometimes the only closure you need is understanding that your future deserves better.

Another thing that forgiveness is not is a requirement to put yourself back in the situation that hurt you. If you forgive a group of former friends for encouraging you to do things that were bad for you, you don't need to revisit or condone those bad behaviors. Forgiveness actually frees you from the situation, because it finally puts the situation in your past. I want you to really connect with that message. Forgiveness is not about saying that what happened to you was right, and it isn't about endorsing a way of dealing with people or the kinds of activities that led to you getting hurt. If a situation hurt you so badly that you're still carrying that pain around with you months or even years later, that is a situation you never want to get near again. Forgiveness definitely doesn't require you to go back to the "scene of the crime." It's about acknowledging that what's done is done and moving past the extreme feelings related to it.

I had an experience like this a bunch of years back. When I first started speaking regularly, I met a young guy who was involved in putting together a few of my speaking events. Those events went well. And because they went well and because he had worked with a few big-name people, he gained my trust. We wound up building a friendship out of it. So I said to him, "Hey man, let's do other cities." Based on our friendship, we made a partnership happen, and we started to tour cities. As promoter, he would take care of everything and then pay me what I was owed. But then I discovered that this was his first time really doing something this big, and he didn't know how to manage the money right.

Eventually, at one point during the tour, I was no longer getting paid because he'd mismanaged the money. The tour still had to go on, but he dropped out of it and I had to take on the burden of making things right with people. I had to take care of payments and pick up all the slack. Meanwhile, this guy owed me thousands of dollars that I never saw. And he never tried to make it right.

That really put me in a bad place as far as trusting people in business—with trusting anybody, really. That someone I knew and had built a friendship with could do this to me made me bitter. I didn't want to work with people. I immediately said no to any proposition that came across the table; I didn't care who the people were. Because of what happened, I saw everybody the same way I saw this guy, thinking they wanted to take my money and use my name for their own profit.

Over time I realized that I was making other people pay for mistakes they didn't make. Everybody wasn't this guy. I had to break that thinking because not only was it messing up my ability to reach and connect with people across the world and with others who had good intentions, it was also messing up my personal life. I started to look at people around me differently, wondering what they wanted from me. I wasn't enjoying life. And I definitely wasn't enjoying speaking because I was so on guard.

I realized I had to forgive my former business partner. This guy was young. He'd never been in that position and had never handled that type of money before. And it wasn't that he'd wanted to steal money; he'd just mismanaged it and didn't know how to make that money back. Forgiving him, even though I never had a conversation directly with him, helped put me in a better place, and I was able to move on with my life and work with other people.

The Three Steps to Forgiveness

I know, real forgiveness isn't as simple as saying, "Okay, I forgive you," right? Definitely not. The kind of forgiveness that has a strong and lasting effect on your life takes quite a bit more than that.

The first step you need to take to get yourself ready to forgive is to soften your heart and get into a better mind state. If you've been carrying around a lot of anger and resentment, even if it's just toward one person, this has been having an effect on your heart and mind. Probably without realizing it, you've become less willing to give your heart to others, and maybe you've become more pessimistic about your life and the world around you. You're not going to be able to truly forgive while you're in that condition. But getting out of that place when you're in it is no easy task. Fortunately, we've been working together on this sort of thing for a while now, so you have some tools available. Remember when we talked about owning your darkest moments in chapter 3? You might want to go back to that section now to run through that exercise again. Really taking ownership of what happened to you will come in handy now. So will understanding that your pain has a purpose, which we also talked about in chapter 3. You might also want to think again about how much your future matters to you, which we talked about in chapter 4. These are the kinds of exercises that can help you fine-tune your mind state and put you in a place where your heart is open to forgiveness.

The next step is to ask yourself, "Do I want this grudge to control the rest of my life?" As we talked about earlier, when you hold on to your anger and resentment, you're letting someone who does not love you have a serious amount of control over you. It's affecting how you relate to your family. It's affecting how you relate to your friends. It may even be preventing you from falling in love or getting ahead in your job. I don't think we truly appreciate how much old grudges hurt us until we isolate them. Can you see a direct connection between what happened to you when you were hurt and what has happened to you since? Are you less enthusiastic, less optimistic, less loving, less trusting—*all because of this?*

That's a crazy amount of control that you're giving over to someone who probably isn't even in your life anymore. That's tough, but at least you're aware of it now. So, then, the question becomes whether or not you're okay with continuing to give away this kind of control. Since you've gotten this far in this process, I'm guessing your answer is no.

Great. So now you have your head and heart in the right place, and you're resolved to not let this old grudge control you any longer. Now, all you have to do is commit.

There are a number of ways you can go about this. One is to have a really honest conversation with yourself about what happened, what the circumstances were, what the other person's intentions were, and what it felt like to go through it all. Of course, there's a pretty good chance that the first thing that's going to happen when you have this conversation with yourself is that you're going to get angry all over again, which might feel a little counterproductive. Trust me: I know it sucks to remember things you try so hard to forget. But it's necessary to get the proper understanding so you can move on. Remember that in the last chapter we talked about digging up those bad seeds. This is a step to making sure those seeds no longer grow anything in your life. And that's going to be okay, because you have a better idea now of what that anger is doing to you. And as you continue to talk this out with yourself, now that you've prepared yourself for dealing with it, you're probably going to find that you are ready at last to let it go. Allow yourself to face it. Allow yourself to feel it again—even if that really hurts—and then acknowledge that this has taken way too much space in your life for way too long and that it's time to see it as an unfortunate part of your past that will no longer have an influence on your future.

If you're someone who prays, this is a great thing to pray about. I've found prayer to be extremely helpful to me, and it's often the last step I need to take to get past an old hurt.

Another way to achieve forgiveness is to share everything that happened with a good friend or family member. Sometimes, explaining your feelings to another person changes the power of those feelings. Maybe the person you're sharing this with knows this part of your story already. Or maybe she's never heard any of it before. Either way, speaking about these feelings out loud often blunts their effect, and talking about the situation with someone else can often give you new perspective—even if the person you're telling it to does nothing more than listen. Often, things sound different to you when you say them out loud and you really *hear* them for the first time. And when you finally finish telling your story and you get to the point where you can honestly say, "I'm ready to forgive him for that," this is going to feel like a real breakthrough for you, and you're that much more likely to believe it yourself because you've committed it to another person.

Then there's another option. Remember when I said that forgiveness doesn't require you to ever let the other person know that you've forgiven her? That's absolutely true. However, if you're up for it, confronting the person who hurt you directly can be the most liberating form of forgiveness. First of all, it gives you a real sense of closure to go up to someone, remind her what she did to you, and then say, "I forgive you." You can't really walk that back once you do it, and that's a good thing, because it's critical that you believe that forgiveness is a permanent thing if you're going to get all the benefits from it that you deserve. When you confront the person directly, you also forever change the dynamic of what happened between you. Yes, earlier I said that there was a good chance that the person who hurt you no longer thinks about you at all. But maybe she does, and she's taking a tiny bit of pleasure from having screwed with your life. If you let this person know that it's all behind you, you're probably going to ruin her day, and you can get a little extra satisfaction from that. And on the more productive side, if she does realize what she's done to you and actually feels kind of guilty about it, telling her that you forgive her may actually inspire her to do the extra work necessary to be a better person in the future.

A Little More on Forgiveness Before We Move On

Forgiveness can be a life changer for you, and it might even be one for the person you forgive. It's a huge part of the three-stage process for getting the negative influences out of your life that began with burning bridges and continued with digging up your bad seeds. If you can get yourself to the point where you let go of the anger and resentment you've been carrying around with you, you will be so much closer to becoming the best version of yourself. Before moving on, take a little time to think about these questions to make sure that you've dealt with the key concepts of this chapter:

- What bad situations have you moved on from physically but not emotionally?
- Why do you think the people who hurt you did what they did?
- Are old grudges weighing you down?
- Are unresolved grudges getting in the way of the life you're living now?
- Are you willing to let them continue to have control over you?

By getting this far, you've done a ton of work to set the stage for your future. The next chapters are going to be about doing things that actively make your life better. Let's get started on that right away.

7

PROTECTING
YOUR PEACE

---

t was in 2015 when I realized that I was *on* all of the time. My wife and son were the most important part of my life, so I always wanted to be there for them. And I had to be available for my friends now that I'd dug up all of the bad seeds and left myself surrounded by people who were making my world better. And, of course, I wanted to be there for my followers in every way I possibly could, and by this point, comments and requests were coming in twenty-four hours a day. I easily could have filled every minute I was awake giving myself to all the things I was connected to. This was especially true with social media, where all the time I felt the pull to post something because it seemed as if so many people were depending on me. I needed to offer one person advice; I needed to send another person a message to let her know I was listening; I needed to make a new video to say something about an issue that lots of people were asking about. There was always something, and there was always something *more* that I could do.

I love my family, I love my friends, and I love my followers, and staying connected to all of them is super-important to me. The only thing was that by this point in 2015, it felt like I was connected every single second—and I was exhausted.

I realized the issue was that I wasn't taking time at any point during the day to get myself ready for the day. I had gotten into the habit of reaching for my phone the second I got up, often without even getting out of bed. Does this sound familiar to you? I'm guessing it does, because a whole lot of people I talk to do the same thing. I would wake up and jump right onto social media. I would see posts from people I follow that caused all kinds of reactions in me, both positive and negative. I would see reactions to my posts that required a response—sometimes an immediate response. I would see things that would get me excited or inspired or angry, and I would start acting on them right then. And I was still in bed! And so, my day would start as though I'd been shot out of a cannon. I'd go from fast asleep to full throttle in a matter of minutes, and that would get me so amped up that I couldn't operate at any other level the entire day. Of course, I was burning out. How could I not be? I was starting my day off in stress and then I'd wonder why the rest of my day was stressful. I was using so much mental energy before I got out of bed that I was burned out by eleven in the morning.

When I finally realized how much damage this was doing to me, I made a key decision. I was going to stop reaching for my phone as soon as I opened my eyes. Instead, I was going to get out of bed, thank God, then get dressed and go for a hike. I took to this right away. As I went up into the trails, I would spend time just noticing everything around me. I would get a nice pace going, and I would feel the good clean air filling my lungs. And best of all, my phone didn't work while I was up there, because there was no signal, so I had nothing drawing my attention away from nature. I couldn't connect into my world of distractions, so I had no choice but to let the distractions go. I would always tell myself, "For these forty-five minutes, nothing matters outside these trails. It's my place where worries can't find me, problems can't reach me, and stress can't control me."

About a week after I started doing this, I realized that my days were going much more smoothly after these hikes and that I felt much stronger and was no longer feeling burned out. Sure, I still had a lot to deal with, and there were definitely still hassles and problems that demanded my attention, but I found that these things weren't stressing me out as much and that I was finding better solutions to any difficulties I encountered. The day just worked better when I gave myself a little time to enjoy life first thing in the morning.

What I'd discovered was the enormous value of protecting my peace—making sure that I took care of myself before I jumped into the world. By starting every morning with a peaceful transition into the day, I was reaffirming the part of me where I was strongest and most centered. And by doing this, I went into every day with a tremendous amount of power, more than enough to contend with anything that might come up. I'm still as busy as ever—much busier, actually, than I was in 2015—but I'm not exhausted anymore, because I've found a completely renewable source of strength.

Why Peace Is So Important

I'm guessing you recognized yourself in at least some of my story. I read a report recently that said that 80 percent of smartphone users check their phones before brushing their teeth, so even if you get out of bed before you check yours, there's a good chance that you know what I'm talking about. And even if you aren't jumping on social media the minute your day starts, it's pretty likely that you're throwing yourself right into the world in some other way—rushing the kids off to school, turning on the television to watch the news or some talk show, jumping back into the work you were doing before you went to bed. Does any of this sound like you?

Well, obviously you're not alone, but there's a problem with doing this to yourself. Remember a few chapters back when we were talking about how seeds—both good and bad—are being planted in your life all the time? When you immediately start to interact with the world the second you get up, you're allowing all kinds of seeds to be planted before you've even gotten a chance to get your feet under you. Now, if these were all good seeds, I guess it wouldn't be a problem, but how many of us can put ourselves into the world without coming in contact with any bad seeds at all? You go onto Facebook and see that two of your friends are fighting. You check Twitter and see a bunch of people reacting to some self-important celebrity's crazy tweet. You turn on the news and hear about some kind of tragedy or injustice happening in the world. Maybe none of this happens on any given day, but with all the stuff going on around you all the time, the odds are pretty good that something is going to plant a bad seed in you as soon as you expose yourself.

That means you're essentially playing defense from the minute you wake up. Sure, a day that begins with irritation or concern or worry can still turn around and be a championship day for you, but if that happens, it happens because you've fought your way through the bad start. How much emotional energy do you need to use in order to do that? It's a lot. And if you're being honest with yourself, you can probably think of plenty of days where you were annoyed or alarmed right at the beginning and things stayed that way all day.

And think about it another way: How willing would you be to pick your head up from your pillow and immediately start a conversation with a thousand people? You know, just get out of bed, walk into the next room, and have a thousand people there saying stuff at you and expecting you to respond. That would be insane, right? But that's effectively what you're doing when you jump onto social media first thing. You dive into a conversation with a thousand people, you get all kinds of information, at least some of that information is going to be negative, and you find yourself being drained before you've even brushed your teeth.

Here's what I know: you are always in control of two

things—what you give and what you accept. Let's talk here about the acceptance part. The world is going to present you distractions every day. Things that don't serve you, grow you, or help you. The problem is we accept these things far too often. Protecting your peace will teach you that you don't have to accept anything that doesn't benefit your day.

Things are different when you start your day by protecting your peace. You know how they say that breakfast is the most important meal because getting the right nutrition in you then can power you through your entire day? Well, the same thing is true about "feeding" your peace as your day begins. When you work on protecting your peace first thing, you give yourself the opportunity to appreciate your life, appreciate the people and the world around you, focus on your goals and ambitions, and bolster your inner strength. At the same time, you allow yourself to keep the big stresses in your life away for at least a little while. It's not that you forget that they exist, but you de-prioritize them while you concentrate on the part of your life that gives you the most satisfaction and contentment. It's like wrapping yourself in a powerful protective coating. When you make working on your peace the first item on your agenda and you begin every day with a strong sense of well-being, it is way harder for the distractions and the irritations to throw you out of whack. It's much easier for you to guard your life, to focus on where you want to go and what you want to do with your day. You aren't playing defense the moment you get out of bed. Instead, you get to go on the initiative and score your first points before the opposition even gets to handle the ball. That's the way you win championships.

Giving Yourself Some Tools

So, what exactly do I mean by "protecting your peace"? What I mean is allowing yourself to enter the day with the experience of genuine happiness to be alive. I always start the day by thanking God, though I know that might not be your thing. My hikes made me feel great about the beauty of nature, the world around me, and my place in it, but I use a bunch of different techniques to protect my peace, including walking around the neighborhood, working out, and yoga. I even had this thing where I used to start every day by dunking a basketball, but that was before we got rid of the basketball goal at our house. (Also, to be honest, it was a seven-foot goal, not a ten-foot goal; I mean, I'm a good athlete, but dunking at regulation height is *hard*.) All of this stuff allowed me to fill the beginning of my day with goodness and a strong sense of positivity. It's much easier to feel like you're going to win the day when you start with some winning.

Now, none of the things I do to protect my peace might be the right thing for you, so let's go over the basics. What you're looking for is any routine that offers you a stress-free experience and makes you feel good about your life and your situation. Maybe it's doing some breathing exercises. Maybe it's making a nice breakfast. Maybe it's listening to some uplifting music or picking up a guitar and strumming a few chords. There are people I know who start the day by working on a personal project—some carpentry or writing, for example—and they say that the hour or so they spend at this propels them through the entire day, even if they find their jobs boring or unsatisfying.

There are so many ways to go with this, and as far as I

can see, there are only two real conditions. The first is that it has to be something that always makes you feel good about what you're doing and about yourself. If you have a hobby you love, and you always find yourself getting into the zone when you're doing it, great. However, if that hobby sometimes frustrates you because you aren't as good at it as you feel you should be, don't make this the way you try to protect your peace, because there's a decent chance it's going to generate some stress, and that's exactly what you're trying to avoid at this point. Remember that you're looking for an easy win here, your equivalent of dunking on a seven-foot goal.

The other condition is that you genuinely make this a routine. The difference between doing something to protect your peace occasionally and doing it every day is huge. This was something I learned during my football days. When I was getting ready for a game or for practice, I always prepared myself the same way—getting dressed the same way, stretching the same way, going through my mental checklist the same way. Some might suggest this was a robotic approach to things, but what I found was that preparing like this subconsciously set me up so I was ready to go. The actions themselves were getting me primed. If you get into the routine of doing whatever you choose to do to protect your peace, and you get an emotional boost from this, that emotional boost will be your signal that you can handle anything that comes at you the rest of the day. There's a cumulative effect to this. Doing it every day makes it much, much stronger than it would be if you only did it some of the time. I know that when circumstances make it impossible for me to do my routine on any given day, I can absolutely tell the difference.

Now, protecting your peace doesn't necessarily mean that you have to shut yourself off from the rest of the world while you're doing this. It also doesn't mean that you have to do it entirely alone. Doing something with a loved one or a partner can be a great way to protect your peace. If you and a friend go for a run together first thing, that can really work. Or maybe there's an exercise class that you love going to before you go to your job. During the school year, I'll drive Tristan to school and we'll talk about his goals for the day and how he's going to achieve them. We both get a huge amount out of that, and it always gets my day off to a great start.

The only challenge that comes with protecting your peace with someone else is avoiding things that *don't* protect your peace. If going for that run with your friend requires you to text her to make sure she's ready and then you decide to spend a little time on Snapchat since you already have your phone out, come up with some other way to make your plans. If going to the exercise class means you need to drive through heavy traffic and that stresses you out, maybe working out at home before going to work makes more sense. When I'm driving Tristan to school, I always keep the conversation positive. This isn't the time to fill his head with doubts or warnings. Protecting your peace can be a great thing to do with other people. Just make sure that these people are contributing to your peace and not taking away from it and that you're doing the same for them.

And whether you're protecting your peace by yourself or with someone else, the other key tool is disconnecting. Get into the habit of disconnecting often and regularly. If you're like me and a whole lot of other people in the world, you feel like you're supposed to be available all the time because you *can* be. Your phone always needs to be nearby, and all of your notifications need to be turned on. If the world wants to touch you, you think it should always be able to. Get over that. Be selfish for 5 percent of your day and disconnect completely from the outside world. Anyone who really needs you can get you during the other 95 percent of the time, and just stepping away for a while is extremely important not just for yourself but for those who need you to be the best you.

Rehabber Freya is a single mom of three who had to transition from being a wife to being a provider. For a while, this meant working two jobs and pretty much living to work. When she started her own business, she was able to let go of the second job, but the intensity of her work got way greater. She was doing really good stuff, and she was creating a great home for her kids, but it was a lot.

"I found myself in a space where I was super-drained," she told me. "I was just tired emotionally."

Around this time, Freya came to one of my speaking engagements and completely connected with the importance of protecting her peace.

"I realized that I had to make protecting my peace a priority. The business I'm involved in is a relationship business, so I deal with different personalities, different backgrounds, and different emotions, so I have to be the constant. I can't let the negative things happening around me affect me. And that's what was happening, and it was affecting my business and the way I was treating people."

Freya committed to "starting each day with a fresh start and an attitude of gratitude. It's so easy for us to pick up the phone and check our social media feed, but that can instantly put us in a negative frequency before we even get out of bed. So, I use my first moments waking up—it can range from ten minutes all the way to an hour—thanking God and having a one-on-one talk with Him. I have on inspirational music or motivational audio, or I might even read a couple of pages in a personal development book."

During that speech, I mentioned that hiking was a big help for me, and Freya has picked up on this as well. "When I get to a point of chaos, frustration, and being overwhelmed, I need to go take a hike—literally. Just a time-out to clear my head and refocus."

She will also occasionally practice protecting her peace with someone else by having a prayer partner. "A person I can pray with through these moments can lift and calm whatever it is that has affected me."

The work Freya has done to protect her peace has made a big difference. "I don't force things anymore. I don't force relationships, I don't force situations. And it's made things just flow better for me. Taking that time in the morning to talk to God, or listen to inspirational/motivational audio, or read a book—just waking up grateful—has totally switched things up.

"You have to be selfish with yourself. Especially when you have goals. Especially when you want to impact lives."

Developing Positive Boundaries

There are lots of benefits to protecting your peace. Definitely the greatest of these is the frame of mind it puts you in for the rest of the day. It's way, way better to start your day with something that is guaranteed to make you feel good than to start it with something that is likely to cause you stress and plant some bad seeds in your life. Another huge benefit is that getting in the habit of protecting your peace when you start your day also teaches you how to develop positive boundaries in your life.

As we've discussed in this chapter and all over this book, all of us get lots of input into our lives all the time. We get people coming at us from every direction with all kinds of intentions and expectations. It is way easier for us to be influenced by all of this input than most of us would like to admit, and probably much more of it is getting through to us than we realize. We all know people who get under our skin, who can change our mood in a second, who can make us react in a way we don't like or make us do things we don't really want to do. Since we've been working together for a lot of time now, you probably have fewer and fewer of these people influencing you. But you probably still have some, and you never know when a new one is going to pop up. Here's where the second benefit of protecting your peace comes in handy.

What you've done to protect your peace is put up a boundary between yourself and anything that might take away from your peace when you start your day. This gives you that protective coating I was talking about earlier. It's essential that you do this when you wake up for the reasons we've already discussed. But that boundary-building skill is also an extremely powerful and valuable tool that you can use whenever you need it.

At some point in any day, you're going to have to start interacting with the world. Not many of us can stay isolated all the time, and it wouldn't be healthy if we could. But interacting with the world means interacting with things, people, and situations that are going to take away from our peace. Some of this is unavoidable, but a lot of it can be minimized by using the tools that you're already using to start your day.

For example, you've cut out social media first thing in the morning because you know that it gets you riled up. If that boundary is working for you, then extend that boundary. Unplug from the internet more often, or at least make sure to do so during times when you're most vulnerable, like when you're tired or hungry. If taking a walk around the neighborhood is a tool you're using to protect your peace in the morning and you have a high-stress job, maybe you want to bring that boundary along with you and go for a quick walk at lunchtime before getting back to work. The key to setting up healthy boundaries that extend into the world is to take a good look at what works well for you when you're protecting your peace. What are you protecting yourself from? How often can you avoid this during the rest of the day? What are you using as a form of protection? How do you take that with you wherever you're going?

You're going to find that the things you do to protect your peace are extremely "portable." You can take most of it with you into the world and use it when you need an emotional boost—and to reinforce the boundaries that you've successfully established to get your day off to the best possible start.

One more thing about boundaries: they don't by their nature push people away—at least not the right people. Boundaries serve the purpose of letting yourself and others know what is and isn't acceptable in terms of reaching into your life. If you let others know that you're not okay with trash-talking friends or texting in the middle of the night, some people might have a problem with that, but those aren't people you want in your life, anyway. Everybody else will understand that this is part of the package that comes with being associated with you, and they'll respect you for that. So, if you say to someone, "Sorry. I'm only going to be checking Facebook twice a day from now on," or, "You know, I think I'm just going to sit at my desk and listen to quiet music instead of going out to lunch with the group," you don't have to worry that doing this is going to make you seem unfriendly or standoffish. In general, people respond really well to other people's boundaries, as long as they understand that this isn't a reflection of how you feel about them. So, use your boundaries effectively, and you can protect your peace for most of the day.

Taking It to the Next Level

There's really nothing you can do wrong when you're protecting your peace other than letting someone or something interfere with your process. Whatever method works for you and gives you a strong sense of positivity going into the day will do the job. However, there are things you can do to take this to another level.

One thing would be to supplement whatever you're doing with affirmations. Remember that the goal here is to put yourself in a good place for the rest of the day. You want this first period after you wake to leave you convinced that you're going to go out there and win. Since that's the case, it's a good idea to remind yourself of what the best you is like.

So when you're in the process of protecting your peace, repeat to yourself the things about you that make you feel most optimistic about yourself. Recount your recent wins, whether it be getting a compliment at work, having an important conversation in a relationship, doing things to make yourself better physically, getting closer to an important goal, or whatever. List your personal traits about which you're proudest—things like being persistent, being a good friend, being responsible, or maybe being capable of working through the first six steps in this book. Then list all of those you're in the process of improving: "I'm becoming a better parent," "I'm taking more responsibility for my life," "I'm making better decisions about who I let in and who I keep out," and so on. By incorporating this into whatever you're doing to protect your peace, you're giving this experience more direction; you're giving yourself another protective layer, this time composed of all the ways you're moving forward with your life.

Another way you can make protecting your peace more valuable is by aligning it with your purpose. By this point, I'm hoping you have a good sense of what your purpose is, even if you didn't have any idea of it before you started reading this book. Remember that your purpose is who you are, so it makes sense that aligning your purpose with your peace would lead to a very powerful start to any day.

So, what does this mean? You might be thinking, *My purpose and my peace are two completely different things. My purpose is to help people in crisis, but the thing I do to protect my peace is spend the first half hour of the day sitting on my porch, listening to the birds.* Now, I'll admit that those two things do seem to be very different, but you can still bring them together. Maybe it's by reminding yourself that this half hour with the birds is supercharging you for a day of bringing others the peace you're feeling now. Maybe it's by remembering times you have previously helped people in crisis and carrying some of that joy with you while you're spending time with nature.

The goal here is to make the experience of protecting your peace as rich and restorative as possible. When you connect that peace with the goals for the rest of your day, you get as much out of this as you possibly can.

And ultimately what you're shooting for here is a way to make yourself superstrong for every day. When Tristan and I are driving to his school, I talk to him about how he's going to make this day a championship day. That's what I want you to be thinking about every morning. What are you going to do from the time you wake up to the time you go back to bed that will make you feel like a champion? Protecting your peace is a really important tool because it helps you to keep the world from planting too many bad seeds in you. But it also has an objective: to give you the armor you need to put the absolute best version of yourself out there. As we've been discussing in this book, the greatest you is going to be taking an awful lot of chances. When you start your day by protecting your peace, you make yourself fully capable of making the most of those chances.

Some Questions

As you can see, in this chapter we've moved from the work of getting the negatives out of your life to adding positives into your life. We're going to do more of that in the next chapter, but before we move on, I'd like you to take some time to answer these questions to make sure you have a good sense of what protecting your peace is all about:

- How quickly do you start to let the rest of the world in after you wake up in the morning?
- Do you regularly find yourself feeling stressed or overwhelmed early in the day?
- What are the things that bring you the most peace?
- How can you work these things into a routine right after you get out of bed?
- What does a championship day look like to you, and how can you use the tools you use to protect your peace to help you win more often?

Give yourself a little time to answer these questions, then follow me into the next chapter, where we're going to start talking about the long game in your life.

8

THE CHAMPIONSHIP
MIND-SET

One of my greatest experiences in professional football was getting to work with Peyton Manning. Anytime you have the opportunity to share the field with a Hall of Fame quarterback, it's special. But through the way he conducted himself, Peyton taught me about a lot more than football.

Probably the biggest lesson came one day at practice. We were running a pass play, and Peyton made a great pass and we scored. We were all feeling good about that, but Peyton quickly called us back together to run the play again. The receiver who caught the ball said, "Why do we need to run it again? We just scored." Peyton's answer was as direct as it could be: "It wasn't perfect." He pointed out that the receiver had run the route too deep, which meant that Peyton had to make an adjustment that he might not be able to make at game speed. If Peyton had thrown the ball to the spot where the receiver was supposed to be, the pass would have been incomplete. In fact, it might even have been intercepted. So, while the rest of us were celebrating the fact that we'd scored in practice, Peyton was focusing on the point of the practice—to be great in games. That's the reason why he won two Super Bowl MVPs and is considered one of the greatest quarterbacks of all time. He was always preparing to perform at the absolute best level by practicing the skills that get you there.

What I learned from Peyton right then is something that I've been able to apply to life in general: when you practice being your best every single day, you're going to be your best. I call it the championship mind-set, and now that you've done all the work you've already done in this book, it's time for you to make that mind-set your own.

To me, there are five traits associated with the championship mind-set: *commitment, discipline, consistency, faith,* and *heart.* If you have all five working for you to the best of your ability, you're going to win. It's as simple as that.

Let's take a look at each of these traits.

1. Commitment

Let's get this out of the way right up front. Do you know what the opposite of the championship mind-set is? It's something I call the New Year's mind-set. I'm sure you know what I'm talking about. That's when the New Year comes around and you make all kinds of resolutions about how you're going to make your life better. Then, for the next couple of weeks after that, you take those resolutions seriously. You eat better; you work out more; you push yourself a little harder at work; you attempt to be a better friend, a better communicator, and better at your relationships. Then, somewhere around the third week of January, you start to slack off. The new diet didn't cause you to drop twenty pounds in ten days, so what's the point? You wake up too tired to work out, so you skip it. A friend says something to tick you off, so you go back to throwing shade online.

We've all been there. Every New Year, you promise you're going to "fix" yourself, but when the results of the changes you've made don't come fast enough, you bail. I totally get it, but there are two serious problems with this approach. One is that very few important changes happen overnight. If you're going to get in better shape, you don't go from being a couch potato to an Olympic athlete in a few days. Anything that requires a real change in you is going to require a real commitment from you. You have to understand that no change is possible without a serious commitment.

Commitment is all about staying true to what you said you were going to do, long after the mood you had when you originally said it has left you. I think most people truly want to make the changes they say they want to make to improve their lives. They're just not prepared to deal with what happens when the plan runs into a roadblock. Let's be serious about this: real life is full of roadblocks. People don't decide they're going to improve themselves and then follow a straight path to improvement. Just being totally honest about it, the journey of change sucks, but those who can stay committed to the journey will find it incredibly rewarding. Remember what I've been saying throughout this book: you've gotta work at it. Sometimes, you put in the work and you get a great payback. For example, you decide you're going to lose weight, you start a new diet, and a week later you've lost five pounds. It's easy to stick with a program when the results are right there in front of you. But what are you going to do when you eat all the right things, you deny yourself that big bowl of ice cream, and you still wind up gaining a pound? We all know that happens, right? Is that the point when you throw in the towel and head for the freezer, or is that when you power through, telling yourself that you know this new diet is the best thing for you and that the results will be there over time?

That's what commitment is about. It's about sticking with the things you know are right for you, even when the evidence seems to be to the contrary. Champions commit. They decide what's important to them, they put together a plan, and they stick to that plan regardless of what the results of that plan might be from day to day.

Rehabber Lori showed an intense amount of commitment when she made the decision to help people battle addiction and depression. She'd fought her own battle with addiction, and she was devastated to discover how serious the addiction problem was in her community.

"Something terrible was happening in the area where I lived, and I started feeling a fire burning inside me to do something about it," she told me. "I learned of three people from my high school who had died from heroin overdoses, and I realized that a drug epidemic was forming."

Lori knew that getting into treatment without insurance was a major problem, but she was convinced that she could find ways to help others with this. Though she had no experience putting on community events, Lori was committed to making a difference for this cause, so she got her old high school to let her use the school and she reached out to the PTA for assistance.

"I had no idea how the event was supposed to look, but I knew I had to do it. While I was planning, someone from the PTA asked if I had considered turning my efforts into a 501(c)(3) nonprofit organization. At first, I said no, but then I did some research and found how I could."

Lori named her organization after military personnel, because she believed that you had to think like a soldier to battle addiction and depression. She held that first event, and 185 people showed up. It was a definite success, and Lori could have left it at that, knowing that she'd helped raise some awareness. But she was committed to doing way more than that, so she kicked it up to the next gear.

"My audiences grew from 185, to 300, to 700, to 1,000, to more than 1,000."

She was making a real difference with her organization, but then her commitment was seriously tested.

"The most unimaginable pain hit me when I found out my best friend, and someone I had helped since the beginning, had died from an overdose. I was so lost after my friend died that I got to a point where I considered suicide."

If Lori had been anything less than fully committed at this point, she would have fallen apart. But because she was so committed to this purpose, she came down from the ledge, kept moving forward, and didn't let anything hold her back. Her organization kept growing, she appeared in an MTV documentary with celebrities and political figures, and she was invited to the White House twice.

"I have my dream career, and I am still active in the community. I found purpose, and now I get to help others do the same."

Doing what Lori did required championship-level commitment. So, how do you get better at commitment? You do it the same way Peyton and the Colts got better on the field—by practicing until you're perfect at it. Like all of the other traits associated with the championship mind-set, you can practice your way toward perfection at commitment. It's all about turning commitment into "muscle memory."

Muscle memory is what happens when you perform a physical act so often and so well that it becomes automatic for you. A dancer can make a move that seems impossible to most of us because she's practiced it over and over and over again until her body just seems to do it on its own. Mind-set can work exactly the same way. When you practice a mind-set over and over and over, you don't even need to think about it anymore; you just do it, because it's part of you.

The other thing about muscle memory is that you don't want to start to develop it when the stakes are highest. That dancer didn't practice that move for the first time in front of thousands of people. She did it on her own, maybe at half speed, for a long time before she ever tried it in front of a crowd. If you're going to develop great muscle memory with commitment, don't start with something huge, like changing your relationships or trying to learn a new skill. Get into the practice of it first. Take something where the stakes are low. For example, yoga. The stakes here aren't gigantic. Yes, you've heard that yoga can make you healthier and more peaceful, and you know it would be great if you were healthier and more peaceful, but your life isn't going to come crashing down around you if it turns out yoga isn't your thing. But since the idea here is to practice, sticking with it has tremendous value. So, you agree to go to a few classes, and at first things are going okay. Yeah, you're making your body do things that you're not used to doing, but you can see why people like this. Then, after your third class, you tweak something, and you wake up the next day feeling really sore. You start questioning the value of this, because if it's supposed to make you healthier, how come your back is killing you? That's when you have to push through. You have to get yourself to more classes and really give this thing a try. Maybe you're still hurting after the next class, but the class after that goes a lot better, and a couple of weeks in, you feel better than you've felt in a long time. Maybe right after that you hit another wall because your instructor is encouraging you to push yourself, but you break through that one as well. Soon, yoga has a really good place in your life, and you can't wait to get to your next class.

Now, obviously, this is not about improving your life by spending more time taking up yoga. It's about getting into building up your commitment muscle memory. Doing this low-stakes thing and sticking with it even on the worst days will do something extremely important for you: it will show you how to master the mechanics of commitment. Then, when you decide that you need to commit to that new diet, that new skill, that new way of dealing with your relationships, you call on those mechanics when you come to a roadblock. You gain a pound even though you ate well the day before? You can handle it and stick with your plan, because you've already become a pro at commitment.

2. Discipline

You know when I said earlier in this book that lots of things are going to come along to put roadblocks in your life? Well, the same is true with temptation. We get tempted all the time in our lives. There are always opportunities for us to hang with the wrong kinds of people, stay out a little later, or eat that extra piece of cake. These things are tempting because you really want to do them, even though you know they're not good for you and that there's a good chance you're going to pay for doing them later. They feel great in the moment, but they don't get you any closer to being the person you really want to be.

That's where discipline comes in. My definition of discipline is saying no to anything that doesn't get you a yes. In other words, it's denying yourself the things that are going to keep you from being the best version of yourself. That group that you're tempted to hang with can be a lot of fun, but they're not helping you be the greatest you because they're reinforcing behaviors that take you further from your goals. That's not a yes, so you need to tell them no. Staying out later means the party just keeps on going, but it also means you're a wreck in the morning, which messes with your career goals. That's not a yes, so you need to say no. That extra piece of cake will definitely be delicious, but it's also going to set you back in your mission to lose ten pounds before the summer. That's not a yes, so you need to say no.

Discipline is all about exercising self-control when self-control will keep you on track. It's not about saying no to things that you would automatically say no to anyway. It's about understanding what I like to call P.O.P.—Purpose over Pleasure. Just because it feels good doesn't mean it is good. An important question I always ask myself to help me stay disciplined is, "Forty-eight hours from now, am I going to regret making this decision?" For instance, if you don't like the taste of alcohol, turning down a drink doesn't count as discipline because you never wanted the drink in the first place. Yes, turning it down was a good thing because drinking too much can lead to problems, but that's really not an issue for you since you don't like drinking anyway. That second piece of cake, though, that's a whole other story.

Sometimes, it takes a huge amount of discipline to keep yourself on track. Some of the changes we've already talked about in this book are going to be very big changes in your life, and they are going to demand a lot of discipline from you. But remember that getting into the championship mind-set is all about being great in practice so you can be great in the game. So, what you want to do is start practicing at discipline right now. As with commitment, start with something where the stakes aren't too high for you. For example, as I'm writing this, I'm practicing a plant-based diet because I think there might be some health benefits to it. Now, I'm already pretty careful about what I put in my body, so this isn't a high-stakes undertaking for me. At the same time, it definitely takes discipline because I love the taste of meat. I'm not sure that

I'll wind up being on a plant-based diet long term, but this is great discipline practice for me, and I already know that this kind of practice made a big difference when I had to exercise serious discipline at other times in my life, like when I had to move on from that group of people who were dragging me down even though I loved going out with them.

Now, since we're at this point in the book, it's very possible that you've already started on a big change in some part of your life. If so, that's great—keep at it! If you're still getting started though, get some practice at discipline by picking something fairly small that you'd rather not deny yourself but that you know you *should* deny yourself. Get used to saying no to things that don't get you a yes, and you'll develop the muscle memory that you'll use to say no to something bigger when it really counts.

3. Consistency

Let's go back to the football field for a minute. If you follow football at all, you've probably seen players for your favorite team who look great one week and disappear the next. There's that running back who goes for more than a hundred yards a couple of times a year, but has a tough time breaking fifty in the other games. There's that defensive back who will do a great job against a Pro Bowl receiver and then give up two long touchdowns in his team's next game. It isn't that these players lack talent. Some players who fit this description have elite talent. But what they lack is consistency. They're not able to deliver their best performance over and over again.

On the other hand, you'll see people do much, much more with considerably less raw talent. This kind of thing happens all the time. That person at the office who you can always rely on might not be the smartest or the most well-spoken or the most polished person you've ever met, but she always delivers excellent work, and she's the go-to person when the stakes are highest. She doesn't have world-class talent, but she has world-class consistency, and that's taking her further than many others who have more raw talent than she has.

I see this in my own field. I don't think I'm the most talented speaker in the world. I've seen some speakers out there who will blow me away on any given day. But I think I am absolutely one of the most consistent when it comes to living my purpose and providing people with a message they can rely on. Look at it this way: if I started this book by inspiring you to become the best version of yourself, then switched that message to teaching you how to scam the system, then switched to telling you to give up because life is just too hard, and *then* went back to the be-the-greatest-you message, you'd probably quit this book way before I got to that last part. The message would be so inconsistent that you'd know you couldn't count on me for anything. And if you were that inconsistent, the world would soon start perceiving you the same way.

Think about your favorite places to go. Do you have a favorite restaurant? If you do, that place is probably your favorite because you know you're always going to get a great meal there. If the food was fantastic sometimes while other times it was only okay and occasionally it was really bad, you probably wouldn't want to keep going there, right? It's the consistency of the place that makes you love it.

And when I'm talking about consistency with the championship mind-set, I'm talking about being consistently great. Being consistently bad at something important in your life isn't going to help, obviously. And neither is being consistently pretty good. Sure, you're not going to be great at everything you do all the time, but you need to strive to be consistently great at all of the stuff that really matters. What are those things in your world? Is it parenting? Is it your job? Is it helping out in the community? Whatever those things are—and at this point in the book, you should have a pretty good idea—you need to make sure you're consistently at the top of your game. People should never have to wonder what they're going to get from you or who you are going to be from day to day.

How do you practice being consistently great? It's all about practicing mastery. It's that muscle memory thing again. There's power in *focused* repetition. Repetition builds confidence. And I know confidence is a big part of being great at something. Think about something that you're already really good at doing. Maybe you're really good at using the spreadsheet program on your computer. Well, now focus on one particular part of that program, maybe making charts. Now, get as great at making charts as you possibly can. Watch a bunch of YouTube videos and read everything you can find online about it. Practice this to the point where you're an absolute pro at it and you can make great charts every time. What you're getting from this exercise is the training to be consistently great at everything you put your mind to. And once you've done it on a small scale, you're ready to do it on a much bigger scale.

4. Faith

The fourth trait associated with the championship mind-set is faith. Now, when I'm talking about faith, I'm not talking about showing up at your place of worship once a week and going through the motions. I'm talking about a deep, intimate, and unfaltering faith. To me, faith is believing the odds are beatable even when the odds seem impossible. When circumstances are stacked against you, when people are stacked against you, when even *you* are stacked against you, you still believe that you can accomplish what you want to accomplish because you believe that much in what you're trying to accomplish. That's true faith. Faith is believing a door is going to open that doesn't even currently exist.

It required real faith for me to step into the life I have now. Football was over for me (though I wasn't entirely ready to admit it), and I'd started doing the RehabTime videos. But the problem was that I didn't have much of a following, and it stayed that way for a little while. I had a strong sense of faith in what I was doing because I could feel that this was my purpose and because the people I'd been able to touch were genuinely moved by what I was saying. So, I kept at it, even though the numbers weren't there right away. And because I never faltered in my belief that this was the purpose God had for my life, my spirit stayed very strong even though there were lots of things stacked against me.

You know how the rest turned out. But that never would have happened if I'd lost faith when things didn't take off right away. If I'd said to myself, "I don't know; this sounded like a good idea, but things aren't looking so good," and I'd started looking for other ways to make a living, even if those things had nothing to do with my purpose, I would be a compromised version of myself now. But I trusted in God, and I trusted in my journey, and I kept believing in what I was doing even though the odds were pretty terrible. That's what faith is all about.

I've known Brandy for many years now, and if it wasn't for her faith, lots of things would be different. She was born into a family with a history of drug addiction, domestic violence, and sexual abuse, and by the time she was a teenager, she was drinking, doing drugs, and in a physically abusive relationship. She had two children in her late teens and stayed in an abusive marriage for thirteen years before eventually divorcing her husband.

Two years later, Brandy married a man she'd known since high school. But the marriage started to go badly almost immediately. "About two weeks after we were married, he became very verbally and physically abusive," she told me. "He broke me down so low that I no longer could even recognize myself. I tried so hard to fix him, and I made that my goal every day. When he became physically abusive to my sons, I knew something had to change. I moved my sons in with my mother because I knew that they would be safe, and he agreed to allow me to do that. He really just wanted me to himself. The physical abuse got worse. It would happen almost every day. And I just would remember so many times wishing he would just end it all for me."

Things came to a head for her when her husband came home one night drunk and high on drugs and cried to her to call EMS because he thought he was going to die. "I remember at that moment thinking, 'Should I call EMS, or should I just let him die?' I loved who he was, but I hated who he had become."

In the middle of trying to figure out what to do, Brandy saw one of my tweets, and it inspired something in her. "It reminded me that my life was worth it no matter what was going on around me or happening to me. And that there can always be better if I choose better."

She got help for her husband that night, and she also resolved to get herself out of that relationship. From there, Brandy's faith in herself began to grow. "It sparked in me a belief in myself and that one day it would get better. That was a hard journey for me. It was one step at a time, then one day at a time, then one month at a time. What encouraged me was to look back on how far I'd come. Even if it was just one step, it was still a step forward. Every step took faith. I took a lot of faith steps."

Not long after that, Brandy started working for an organization that helped others, and she started living with a greater sense of purpose than she'd ever had before. But there were some big tests of her faith still in front of her. Two big crises slammed her at the same time. One was that her son, at that point a teenager, began to get in a lot of trouble, started hallucinating, became very withdrawn, and would become easily agitated. At first, Brandy thought he was having issues with drugs, but it turned out he was beginning to show signs of schizophrenia. At the same time, some people at her work turned out to be less-than-positive influences on what the organization was doing. Things got so bad that the founder had to take a step back to figure out the organization's next moves.

This combination of things put Brandy in a tough place. She was very worried about her son, and her work had become such an important part of her life that the possibility of it being in trouble was devastating to her. Brandy had already shown that she had a championship level of faith just to get to this point in her life, but now she had to double down.

"At that moment, instead of me being knocked down and staying down, instead of me giving in to everything that was going to take me out, I decided that I was going to get in the game. I didn't want to lay down and die anymore. I didn't want to hide my life anymore, like I had so many times in the past. I didn't know where it was going, but I knew that if there was an entrance, there was an exit. It didn't matter what that thing looked like. It just mattered that we got there."

Brandy had faith that there was a better outcome for her story, even when all evidence suggested that this wasn't the case. And her faith—and her complete devotion to that faith—has been rewarded. The organization she works for got over its hurdles and her family is in a very good place too.

"Both of my sons are well and doing great, and even when we encounter hard times, we know that there is always light at the end of the tunnel. We've learned that sometimes you have to go through places you don't understand to get to the place you need to be."

Dr. Tony Evans says that "faith is in your feet." What he means is that faith isn't about *saying* you believe in your dreams; it's about walking the journey to your dreams. Prayer and confession are great things, and they can have an important place in our lives, but when we take confident steps toward our journey, we're making real strides toward those dreams. If you're going to have a championship mind-set, you need to have a dream that you want to pursue with everything you have, and then you need to maintain the faith that you can get there, even when things go wrong, even when people start telling you it isn't going to work out, and even when you question whether you can succeed.

Like the other traits of the championship mind-set, faith is vital to dealing with the biggest stuff in your life and becoming the best you. But you can practice faith on a smaller scale as well, and that will get you into the habit of making your faith strong enough to overcome all your challenges. Start by doing something that you've always wanted to do—but not necessarily something that would change the course of your life. Maybe you want to get to level 10 on the elliptical at the gym even though you've never been able to get past level 5. This is a great way to practice faith. First off, ask yourself if you really want it. If you don't really want it, then you're never going to be able to muster enough faith to achieve it. But if you *do* want it, then go about getting it. The odds probably don't seem great, right? I mean, you've never gotten past level 5, and level 10 is way harder than level 5. And if you tell your friends that you're shooting for level 10, you know at least a few of them are going to tell you that they think you're not cut out for it. And your body is definitely going to fight you on this one, making even getting to level 6 seem like climbing Mount Everest.

But you want this, remember? You really want it, or you wouldn't have put your faith in it in the first place. Well, now you need to go all in with your faith. You need to keep believing that the odds against you are beatable even though it seems as though the odds are completely against you. And when you get to level 10—whatever your version of level 10 might be—you'll have mastered a trait that you can call on to win even the toughest championships.

5. Heart

We all face situations in our lives where all of our instincts are telling us to give up. You've been trying to fix a relationship, and nothing seems to be getting any better. You've been working on a project for months, and you aren't making any progress with it. You're trying to improve your health, but you keep surrendering to temptation or there are a lot of days where you can't get off the couch. That's when you hear the voice in your head that says, *This just isn't gonna happen*. You start to convince yourself that the best decision is to cut your losses. You gave it your best shot, you think, but it simply wasn't meant to be. Maybe you just don't have it in you, or maybe the circumstances are working against you. Whatever the reason, you're not going to get to that goal.

Before you even think about giving up on something, you've got to ask yourself an all-important question: "Is doing this going to help me become the greatest me?" If the answer is no, then maybe moving on is the right thing. That's what happened with me and football—at some point I realized that football wasn't helping me become who I was supposed to become; it wasn't getting me to my purpose. But if the thing we're talking about matters to you at all and is going to contribute to your being the greatest you, quitting is not the answer. Instead, what you need to do is use heart.

Heart is finding the strength to give more even when everything indicates that you have nothing left. I'm sure it's pretty obvious why heart is one of the five traits of the championship mind-set. After all, championships are not easy to win, and no one is going to make them easy for you. You're going to face a lot of challenges, and some of those challenges will seem like they're getting the best of you. That's when you have to tap into reserves that you might not have even known you had.

Let's look at a couple of the scenarios we were talking about at the beginning of this section. You have a relationship that isn't working out right, and six months ago you decided that you needed to try to find a way to fix it. Maybe you make yourself more open to the other person's needs, or you try to make more time for the two of you to just enjoy being together. But now you're six months in, and there's still a lot of dysfunction and bad feeling in this relationship. It really seems like it's as bad as it's ever been. You take an honest look, and you're convinced that you've given it everything you've got. But have you really given it *everything*? In your mind, you're 99 percent sure the relationship can't be saved. But you know that this relationship was really good once, and you really want it to be good again. What if you tried some things you hadn't considered before? What if you keep doing what you're doing? Sometimes, when there's a lot of damage in a relationship, it takes a long time for the other party to regain trust. Maybe if you keep trying, that trust will develop, and all of the work you've put in will be rewarded. It's going to take a lot of heart, but you have it in you.

Now, let's look at that project. Maybe it has something

to do with your kid's school and it requires getting a bunch of parents together to help. A couple of them are on board, but a few of them won't commit, and most of them aren't even responding to your emails. It's getting late in the school year, and this is looking pretty hopeless. Your head is telling you that you should probably just give up; maybe you can try again next year. But you also know that this thing would be really good for your kid and for all the other kids in her class. Sometimes when people don't join you in a project, it's because they don't understand what the project entails or how it's really going to happen. So, even though you think you've tried dealing with it from every angle, you come up with a new way of getting your message across. Maybe if you figure out a different way to share your enthusiasm, people will help you bring this to life. It takes heart to see something in a new way when you feel like you've already looked at it in every way possible. But you have it in you.

Or maybe the issue is getting yourself to the gym. Your doctor is telling you that you need to get in better shape, and you know that you don't feel as good as you should be feeling. And for a couple of months, you've been going to the gym regularly, making yourself get out of bed early even though you really want to hit the snooze button. But you haven't lost much weight, you're convinced that you look flabby, and you still get out of breath walking up a flight of stairs. If you're going to feel miserable getting out of bed early and working out, you might as well feel miserable and stay in bed, right? But you really don't want to spend the rest of your life feeling miserable, and you've heard that getting in shape often comes in stages. If you keep pushing yourself out of bed in the morning, and you keep putting in your work at the gym, maybe you'll hit a new plateau in the near future, and then the rewards will really start kicking in. It's going to take heart not to go back to sleep, but you have it in you.

Practicing heart is about getting into a mind-set where if you're going to do something, you're not going to give up on it until you get it done. Quitting cannot be an option. It cannot even be a consideration when you're on the road toward being the best you. I'm constantly throwing myself challenges to strengthen my heart. For example, as I'm writing this, I'm training to run the New York City marathon. Why? Because I believe the only impossibilities are the ones you create. I believe that it's not our capabilities that hold us back; it's our mind-sets. I want to prove that theory true. Now, I've been a professional athlete, but running a marathon is something I had never done before. And it is *tough*. I am pushing my body to the limit, and there are plenty of times when I feel like I can't go another step. But my heart is telling me to keep pushing.

There's a thing that marathoners talk about that works as a great metaphor here. What they say is that there comes a point running extreme distances when you hit a wall—many of them say this happens around mile seventeen or eighteen. You're used up, you're having trouble breathing, and your brain starts screaming at you that if you keep going you'll wind up being taken away in an ambulance. But once you get over the wall, you tap into a whole other level of strength that you never knew you had. And that strength is going to take you to the finish line.

With any challenge, there's a good chance you're going to

wind up hitting a wall. That's when your heart is tested. Do you believe that there's a whole other level of strength on the other side of that wall? If you have the championship mind-set, you do. You just need to get some practice at putting it to use.

Remember That Your Life Is Bigger Than You

When the five traits of the championship mind-set become muscle memory, you'll be carrying yourself like a champion and approaching every day the way a champion does. There's one more thing that goes along with this: the understanding that your life is bigger than you. This is a really important concept, and we're going to get into it in depth in chapter 10, but it has particular relevance when we're talking about the championship mind-set. If you're convinced that your life begins and ends with you, then you're probably going to have a hard time adopting the championship mind-set because it's too easy to throw in the towel when you're only living for yourself. I can't stay committed? I'll just have to deal with that. I'm inconsistent? So what? I'm not hurting anybody.

But very few people live lives that don't touch a lot of people around them. Maybe it's your kids, or your family, or your friends, or your community. In all likelihood, it's all of those things. And understanding that we're living for them too is the extra push we all need to convince ourselves to live with a championship mind-set. They need you, and when you win your championship, they're going to be there to help you celebrate.

9

RELATIONSHIPS
ARE EVERYTHING

Eventually, everything comes down to your relationships. When I speak with people about the challenges they're having in their lives, they often first present the problem as being about something else: a job, money, a sense that things are going nowhere for them. But what usually comes out fairly quickly is that the root issue is relationships. The reason a person is frustrated with her job, worried about money, or feels she should be doing more with her life is that there are problems with her most intimate relationship, and that's making everything seem much worse. And this makes sense. After all, if you have a long-term partner, you spend a big chunk of every day with that person. This person forms a major part of your foundation. And if your foundation is shaky, it's hard to build anything on top of it.

On the other hand, if your foundation is extremely strong, the world is going to have an awfully hard time knocking you down. When you have a really good relationship on your side—and this is especially true with marriages—everything else seems conquerable because you always have something good and substantial to turn to. Now, I'm not saying that you can't make your life work without having a strong relationship; obviously you're completely capable of making it on your own, accomplishing great things, and being the best version of yourself without a partner. The point of this chapter isn't to tell you that you need to rush out, get a relationship, and make sure that it is a great relationship because your life is going to be a disaster if you don't have one. But a strong relationship is a big help in getting through life and in creating a safe and secure space for yourself. And if you're currently in a relationship, you want to make sure that you're doing everything you can to keep that relationship healthy and moving forward.

In my experience, there are five simple strategies that you can use to keep your relationship fresh and strong. Let's get to them.

1. Never Stop Dating

There's nothing better than the beginning of a relationship, right? There's lots of mystery there, you find the other person interesting, there's a ton of electricity between you, and you can't seem to get enough of the other person. Those early dating days are amazing, and every date feels better than the last. You also tend to be on your best behavior because you don't want this good thing to go away.

But then some time passes. And things are still really good, and you care about the other person a lot, but a certain amount of complacency has crept in. You know each other pretty well now, so you aren't making as many discoveries anymore. You feel pretty confident that the other person is going to stick around, so you don't try as hard to make him or her *want* to stick around. You let something that happened at work, or something that happened during your day, or something that happened on social media affect your mood and take up the space between you. In short, you become less like the person that the other person fell in love with.

That's an issue. Because the person you're in a relationship with got into that relationship with you because of who you were when you were first dating. That's the person she fell in love with. That's the person who moved his world so much that he decided he couldn't live without you. The complacent person, the one who isn't trying so hard, isn't nearly as interesting. It doesn't necessarily mean your partner is going to leave, but the odds are definitely going up. And even if your partner doesn't leave, the foundation that the two of you have built is going to be a lot shakier than it was when you were that other person. So, here's some simple advice: you'll rarely lose your companion if you keep doing what it took to win him or her.

In other words, never stop dating, no matter how long you've been together. Keep being the person who was so interesting, such a good partner, that this person fell in love with you and wanted to be with you long term.

I get that it isn't practical to stay in dating mode 100 percent of the time. Stuff comes up. Maybe you have kids now. Maybe you have family responsibilities that are pulling at you. Maybe you've taken on other obligations since you've been together and those obligations demand regular attention that wears you down. But here's the great thing about being with someone who loves you: it doesn't take a lot to remind that person why he or she feels that way. As long as you don't become unfamiliar to your partner, as long as you don't completely stop being the person he or she fell in love with, there's a really good chance your partner will stay in love with you. You don't have to work at this 100 percent of the time. Just make sure you aren't working at it 0 percent of the time.

The easiest way to make sure this happens is to keep making dating an important part of your life. Plan a date night at least once a month and preferably once a week. These don't have to be elaborate things, like a fancy meal or a night at a club. You don't even need to leave your home—a quiet dinner with just the two of you after the kids have gone to bed can be plenty. But the key is to make sure you plan some uninterrupted, focused, quality time with your partner and that you do this regularly and don't let other things get in the way. Do something that shows him that you appreciate him. Do something that reminds her that she's the key to your world. Just the two of you being some version of who you were when you first started dating. Those are the people who fell in love. They are the people who will stay in love as long as they keep showing up. Keep it fresh, and it'll keep going.

2. Communication Is Everything

While date nights are great and can do a lot to keep even long-term relationships feeling new and exciting, there's something essential to keeping your relationship strong that you need to do way more often than once a month or even once a week: communicate. Communication is the oxygen to your relationship. Without it, it will die.

When I talk about communication, I'm talking about it on a number of levels. Obviously, you and your partner need to communicate about the big things. If there's a problem with the kids, the two of you need to talk to make sure you're on the same page and to formulate a plan. If there are serious money issues (or even just semi-serious money issues), you need to discuss these and figure a way out of them. If you're thinking about quitting your job or you really want to move to a different state, these are clearly things that you need to discuss at length with your partner. If you feel that you can't discuss things like this with your partner, you may not have as much of a partnership as you think you have.

But when I talk about communication, I'm also talking about the little things. Asking your partner about her day—and actually listening to the response—sends the message that you're interested in what she's doing and that you're always available to offer an ear or to throw in your support. By making a habit of checking in with each other, you make it clear that the line of communication is always open between you. It's also great practice, in the same way that we talked about practicing the championship mind-set in the last chapter. When you practice keeping your communication open at all times, it makes it easier to have the big conversations or the tough conversations when you need to have them because you're always in touch.

Failure to communicate at the "little" level is in my opinion one of the biggest problems most relationships have. Rather than talking about the day at dinner, you check your phone or watch TV instead. You assume that if the other person wanted to tell you about something happening in his life, he'd bring it up, so you don't ask. When your partner asks about what happened at work today, you respond with "Nothing" or, "The usual" instead of finding something to share. And just as practicing communication puts you in a better place when communication is critical, practicing *not* communicating (which is what you're doing when you don't talk about the little things) prepares you to clam up when you get into a situation where the two of you really need to talk.

The most significant reason that communication is so important is because of what you produce when you fail to communicate with your partner: assumptions. When there's no communication, distance is created. And when distance is created, assumptions tend to fill that gap. If you aren't in the habit of staying in touch on both the little things and the big things, then the two of you start assuming things about the other. He assumes that you don't care about what he's been doing all day. You assume that he has nothing meaningful to say to you. You guess at what the other person thinks about important issues or about your future together rather than knowing, which is what would happen if you talked about it regularly. I'm amazed at how many people tell me that they had no idea what their partner was actually thinking when an issue came along that messed up their relationship. That's because they were assuming what the other person was thinking rather than knowing it.

There are very few cases where assumptions are better than knowing. Assuming your spouse meant Cool Ranch Doritos when she asked you to pick up chips from the grocery store is probably okay. But assuming that your spouse is totally fine with your living situation when she desperately wants to get out of the city can lead to some serious heartbreak down the road. Lots of us prefer to make assumptions because we don't really want to hear what's actually going on, but eventually what's actually going on is going to hit you between the eyes. And if you haven't been communicating, you're going to be in for a huge headache. But if you make it a habit to communicate, everything from what to have for dinner to what to do about your child's failing grades becomes easier to navigate together.

3. Understand That You're a Team

Something I see way more often than I would like, and which always disappoints me when I see it, is when two people care about each other but deal with a problem as if they're opponents. They'll act in ways that aren't in the best interest of the other person; they'll say bad things about each other to friends; they'll actively work to undermine the plans of the other. To tell you the truth, I don't get this. If you're in a relationship, you're supposed to be on the same team. It should never get to the point where the two of you are wearing the same jersey but treating each other like the opposition.

Being in a relationship that lasts, that provides you with a great foundation, and that helps you to be the best version of you means understanding that the two of you are a team. You are in everything you do *together*. Your success or failure is completely interconnected. Each of you gains strength from the strength of the other, and you give your strength to help keep your partner strong. I've been on some great teams over the years—including my marriage—and they always include these traits.

So, how do you make sure that you're a great teammate? First off, you need to make sure that you are your partner's biggest cheerleader. Always. Especially when things aren't going great. When you're at a football game, you don't hear the cheerleaders start ragging on their team when they go down by a couple of touchdowns. If anything, they cheer harder, trying to use their enthusiasm to inspire the team to turn things around. It's the same thing in life with your partner. I regularly see people tell their partners that they support them in a new project—something like starting a business or attempting to lose weight—and then get critical when things don't work out the way they were planned. Suddenly, the person who was saying, "Yeah, baby, I just know you're gonna crush that new gig" is saying stuff like, "You were such an idiot to quit your job to start something new. How are we gonna pay the bills?" And instead of, "You look great to me, but if you want to drop some pounds, I know you can do it," it's, "Lose weight? How are you gonna lose weight when you can't walk past a pie without eating three slices?"

If you've gotten nothing else from this book at this point,

I'm sure you've gotten this point: everybody struggles. All of us run into situations where things aren't working out for us. That's happened to you, and I'm sure it's happened to your partner—and it's going to happen again no matter how much work you do to be the best you. Your partner needs you to be a cheerleader all the time, even when things are going great. But especially when things aren't working out. Yes, you may have had doubts about that new project, but the time to express those doubts has passed. Once it's under way, your partner doesn't need to hear that you thought it was a terrible idea. What she needs to hear from you is that you're completely on her side.

Another thing a great teammate does is support the other's dreams and visions. This goes beyond being a cheerleader. A cheerleader is there to offer encouragement and to maintain or even raise spirits. When you're supporting your partner's dreams and visions, you're doing whatever you can on your end to make those dreams and visions a reality. Say your partner has dreams of becoming a chef and of someday opening a restaurant. If you're really supporting your teammate, you're not only open-minded and encouraging about this idea, but when you realize that he *really* wants to do this, you start finding classes for him at the local community college that can help him learn important skills. You make yourself knowledgeable about the restaurant industry, and you share what you learned with him. You supplement the things you know he's good at—coming up with recipes or devising tasty spice combinations—with things that you might be better at that you know he's going to need. For example, opening a restaurant is going to require raising some money, and it turns out that this is not something your partner has the skills to do well. You, however, know how to make people open their checkbooks, so you talk to him about your plans for getting investors when the time is right.

Too many people act in a way opposite of this, especially if they think their partner's dreams and visions are misguided. It's completely okay, of course, to express your doubts and concerns over a particular path your partner is considering. If the communication line is wide-open between you, then he's going to share his visions with you early. At that point, if you say things like, "Training to be a chef is really hard work" or, "You know, most restaurants go out of business in the first year," that's not only fine, but can be useful to helping your partner decide how much this vision really matters to him. But once he decides that he definitely needs to do this, you can't be doing things to make that dream harder for him to attain, and you certainly can't go into passive-aggressive mode, where you're standing back waiting for him to fail. The time for expressing your doubts is over. Now it's all about support. When I played football, if the coach called a play that I was almost certain wasn't going to work, I didn't run my route half-heartedly because the play was going to fail anyway; I did everything I could to help the play succeed, even though it seemed like a bad idea to me from the start. That's what a teammate does.

The third thing that a great teammate does is pick the other person up when she's down. You should never get joy from seeing your partner hurt. You should never get happiness from seeing her cry. Seeing her weakened shouldn't give you an increased sense of power. This is another thing I see way more than I'd like. One half of a couple stumbles and the other half—sometimes quietly, sometimes not so quietly—takes pleasure in this because it makes them the "superior" partner. That is seriously not healthy, it's going to do damage to your partner in the short term, and it's going to kill your relationship in the long run.

When your partner is down, that's when she needs you the most. That's when she needs you to offer whatever is necessary to help the crisis go away. Does she need to talk it out? Then you need to be there to listen. Is she stuck and having trouble figuring out her next move? Then you need to offer some options that she might be overlooking. Is she worried that whatever she's going through is going to hurt your household or the future you've planned together? Then you need to let her know that the two of you are going to figure it out together and that your household and your future are still solid. You are not stronger when your partner is weaker. If you think you are, get that out of your head right now. The outside world isn't going to celebrate you for it, and your personal life is definitely not at its best when your partner is down. On the other hand, when both of you are in a good place and things are truly humming, then outsiders are envious because the two of you make such a great team. So, your goal should always be to help your partner stay in a good place or get back to a good place if things have started to turn bad.

If you change the way you communicate with your partner, you might see a different version of your partner show up. Sometimes, all a person needs is for someone they love to believe in them. There's no greater feeling than having someone you truly care about show you how much they care about you. You cannot expect to build them up by tearing them down. Your communication with them should build them, not break them. Your words should make them feel empowered.

4. Respect Your Relationship

This follows directly from understanding that you're a team. You don't want to do anything to disrespect or embarrass the person that you're with. This really should go without saying, but it's another one of those things that seems to *need* saying with a lot of people I meet. People will talk about their partners' shortcomings in groups of other people. They'll show them up when they make a mistake. They won't stand up for them when they aren't able to stand up for themselves. They'll roll their eyes or make a snarky comment when the other person is speaking. That's wrong on so many levels. First of all, what does it say about you if you're with a person whom you so obviously don't respect? How does that make you look good? Second, if you love somebody, why are you spending time emphasizing what you don't love about him or her? And, really, what are you hoping to accomplish by doing this? Do you think that your friends will think you're funny or that you're so good for "tolerating" your partner? Do you think they'll think you're doing all of the heavy lifting in the relationship?

I'm sure you've been in the situation where someone has done something like this to you. Maybe it wasn't a romantic partner, but it might have been a friend or a family member. How did it feel to be disrespected? How did it feel to have others see that this person had such little regard for you? It probably didn't feel very good. Then why would you ever want your partner—someone you're supposed to love—to feel this way?

And this extends to doing these things behind your partner's back. Even if your partner doesn't know that you're saying embarrassing things behind his back, he's still being hurt by it, and your relationship is still suffering from it. If you spend an entire lunch telling your friends what an idiot your partner is because he failed at something or because he always messes certain things up, your disrespect is doing him harm because you're influencing how your friends feel about him in a negative way.

The advice I always give to people here is to give exactly what you expect in return. Unless you're really okay with your partner disrespecting you (and even if you were when you started this book, I'd like to believe that you aren't now), don't do it to him.

Instead, constantly reinforce the respect that you have for your relationship. When you're out with others, make it clear that you really like your partner for who he is. Mention something he did recently that made you proud. If he brings up something stupid he did recently, don't reinforce this by saying how stupid you thought he was for doing it. Instead, hold your tongue or maybe even explain how he's usually much better at this sort of thing than he was in this situation.

This also holds for people disrespecting your relationship from the outside. Again, we've all been through this. A friend tells you that you can do so much better than being with the guy you're with. Your sister tells you that she doesn't understand what you see in your man. If you think these people might have a point, that's something that you need to deal with, but right then isn't the time to do that. Right then is the time to let people know that you won't tolerate others taking shots at your relationship.

I'm not saying that you need to give everyone the impression that you think your partner is the most perfect person on the planet. As we've been saying, everyone has flaws, and some of these flaws are bigger than others. If you think your partner's flaws are so big that they're hurting your relationship, then you need to address that and maybe even accept that it's time to end the relationship. But for anything short of that, the flaws are part of what make up your relationship—remember that you have flaws too—and in some way they're part of what you love. And if that's the case, then you need to make it clear to anyone who attempts to disrespect your relationship that you're glad to have him, regardless of his flaws.

5. Build Your Own Little World

This is the poem I spoke to my wife on our wedding day:

> When the world tries to tear us apart,
>   let's never forget this moment.
> Let's never let the external things take away from this
>   internal connection.
> Let's build our own little world where nothing matters
>   except the love we have for each other.

At the beginning of this chapter, I mentioned that the reason a strong relationship is so important is that it gives you a great foundation. The key to making that foundation as sturdy as possible—capable of standing up to anything that you pile on top of it—is building your own little world with your relationship.

Look, we already know that the outside world is a tough

place and that it isn't easy for any of us to make our way through it. We also know that certain parts of the outside world are going to try to take you and those you love down. We've all been through that. That's why it's so important to have a world of your own inside that world, a place where you, your partner, and your kids, if you have any, can be yourselves with your own standards and your own agenda.

I found this to be especially important when I started to do the things that made me more of a public figure. When I'm speaking or making videos or talking to people online, I'm totally out there in the world, and everybody has access to me and can do and say what they're going to do and say. Because of this, my wife and kids and I absolutely needed to have a world that was exclusively ours, a place where we could be ourselves, where the outside world couldn't affect us, and where we could celebrate being a unit. I always say to my kids that at the end of the day, family and God is all you have, and we make sure that we insulate those things from everything outside of our space.

There are a few things you can do to build a world for you and your partner. One thing is establishing a sense of privacy between you. I'm not big on keeping secrets, and I think if you spend a lot of time trying to keep secrets, you're going to be wasting a lot of energy, and there's a good chance that those secrets are going to get out anyway. But keeping things private is something else entirely. It is perfectly fine for you to make it clear to the outside world that certain things in your own world are only to be shared by you and those in that world. For example, if you're thinking about having a child, keeping that between you and your partner until you're ready to announce the pregnancy is not only okay but beneficial. For one thing, it gives your personal world strength because it's something only the two of you share. And for another, it keeps others from weighing in on a decision that should really only be between you and your partner. It doesn't have to be anything nearly this big, either. It could be something like deciding to go meatless three days a week or contemplating getting a new car. When you keep certain things, both big and little, private in your world, your world becomes stronger.

Another key to building your world is to have goals. I'm not talking about your personal goals and aspirations here, but rather goals for your own world. For example, my family has a goal of traveling someplace every quarter. These aren't always big trips—sometimes it's about staying in a hotel a few towns over—but lots of planning and discussion go into meeting this goal, and that's something that is distinctive to our world and that we don't invite the outside world into. Because of this, our world gets a little stronger with every trip we plan. Obviously, your goals could be something totally different. Maybe it's seeing all of your favorite musicians when they come to town. Maybe it's deciding what the best ice cream is within a fifty-mile radius. Maybe it's a fitness goal or a spiritual goal or an educational goal or a binge-watching goal. The nature of the goal isn't particularly important. What's important is that this be a goal that everyone in your little world shares and that stays inside of your inner circle. Again, that makes your world distinctly yours.

Yet another way to build your world is to have traditions. Think of your world as your own little country. Different countries have different holidays and traditions. Most countries celebrate Christmas, but only the United States celebrates the Fourth of July. The same can be true in your "country." Sure, you'll have things that you do with your bigger family or with your friends or with your community, but you have some things that just happen within your world. Maybe it's what you do after you go to church. Maybe it's a particular way of celebrating each other's birthdays. Maybe it's what you always do on the first day of the summer, or the snacks you prepare for the first game of the season, or some random day you've picked out in the middle of February to be your day when everyone plays hooky. As long as the tradition feels special to everyone in your world, and as long as you keep that tradition going, it's going to make what you have between you stronger, and that will make your world stronger.

All of these world-building tools do two absolutely critical things: they create a sense of togetherness, and they create a sense of comfort. They create the sense of togetherness because by doing them you're actively working with your partner to do something as a unit that you're doing *just for you*. If you aren't doing that now, or if you feel like you aren't doing it enough, I strongly encourage you to spend more time at it. You'll be amazed at how strong you feel when you're actively working on togetherness. Meanwhile, comfort is what building your own world is all about. When you have a shared world that has some level of privacy, a clear set of goals, and some strong traditions, you create a place that feels good to be in. You create a "home base," a place where everyone involved knows they can be themselves and be supported.

This book has been all about looking at your situation and making the changes in that situation that give you the best shot of becoming the greatest you. If you've been doing the work we've been discussing in this book, you're probably already seeing some meaningful improvements in your life. Now, if you're in a relationship, make sure that your relationship gives you as solid a foundation as possible by following these five guidelines. I think you'll be amazed at how much better this makes you feel about everything in your life. Great partnerships have an incredible way of doing that.

10

WHAT KIND OF
LEGACY DO YOU
WANT TO LEAVE?

I want to take a second before we get started on this last chapter to congratulate you on the work you've done already. I've been challenging you right from the start, and you've had to take a good, hard look at your life and think about making some serious changes. As you know, I've been through my own version of this process, so I can understand what's been going on in your head as you've been reading this book and making the moves to become the greatest you. That you've stuck with it and that you're going forward with some very important steps in your life is a testament to what you have inside of you. That deserves to be acknowledged.

I truly believe that if you follow the path of this book, you will be well on your way to becoming the best version of yourself. And now that this has begun to happen, it's time to think about something else: What is all of this going to mean in the long term?

If you're like a lot of people I talk to, you're focused on the things that are in your immediate future. Much of your life has been about getting by, or solving the problems right in front of you, or simply making it to the end of the day or the week or the month. But now that you're on your way to becoming your greatest you, you need to set your sights on a different place. You need to start thinking about the legacy you're going to leave.

Getting Off the Cycle

What do I mean when I talk about legacy? I mean the things you do that have a real effect on future generations. Every one of us leaves a legacy of some sort. Maybe it's a small legacy, like a recipe, or a story that gets passed down from generation to generation, or a move to a different town that puts your family's roots down there. It's impossible to pass through this life without having some impact on others, and that impact travels forward, even if it is only in a little way. As long as people are still making your aunt's pie, or talking about the time your second cousin played against Bill Russell, or telling friends about when your great-grandfather decided to settle in Tulsa, their legacy is alive and touching others.

Then, of course, there are the negative legacies. I know

far too many people who are dealing with the negative legacies left to them by abusive or neglectful parents or social circumstances that predisposed them to dysfunction. Even if this isn't your situation, I'm sure you've heard the stories too. The guy who beats his wife and kids grew up in a house where his father beat his wife and kids—and *he* grew up in a house where his father beat his wife and kids. The person who depends on drugs and alcohol to get through the day comes from a long line of people who did the same thing. The person who settles for an unchallenging job rather than trying to be great came from a household where she learned that ambition was for "other people."

You hear about "the cycle" all the time: the cycle of abuse or the cycle of chemical dependency. When people talk about these cycles, they're talking about negative legacies. Since you've come to this book, there's a decent chance that you've dealt with some of this in your own life. Maybe your father smacked you around. Maybe your mother was always telling you that you had to set your sights low. If you look back a few generations, you'll probably discover that your mother and father had experiences similar to the ones they're exposing you to—and that their parents dealt with the same thing. Negative legacies tend to stick around for a while.

But think about how much of an effect those negative legacies have had on you. How much have you been held down by them? How hard have you had to fight to overcome them? Then ask yourself this question: Why would you ever want to impose that on someone else? Why would you ever want that to be your legacy? A big part of the work we've been doing in this book has been about coming to terms with the legacies you've been left—and you can make the conscious decision to have those negative legacies end with you.

Legacies are a lot like relay races. Sometimes, the people running the race before you will leave you in a great position to win. That's terrific, and we're going to get back to that in a minute. Sometimes, though, the people running the race before you pass you the baton in a place where you need to run as hard as you've ever run in your life just to stand a chance of winning. There's a really good chance that this is where you were when the baton was passed to you in your own life. Now, you have a handful of choices. You can jog the race out, deciding that you're too far behind to ever catch up. You can push to gain ground to give the next runner a better shot. Or you can be the racer who runs the race at a completely different level and passes the baton over with a huge lead.

Which of these sounds like the best scenario to you? Since you've gotten this far in this book, I think I know the answer, so let's talk about what that means.

The Gift of a Great Legacy

I'm not saying I'm gonna rule the world or I'm gonna change the world, but I guarantee you that I will spark the brain that will change the world.

—TUPAC

There are people in your life right now who are watching and learning from you. There will be more of these people in your future. And there are generations that will follow you that will be influenced by the time you've spent on this earth. How great would it be if you could leave them with something that boosts their place in the world? How much benefit can the greatest you provide to those who follow? The question I continue to ask myself is this: "If I couldn't say one word, what would my life say?" That question keeps me accountable to make sure I'm not just talking the change, but actually making the change. It's easy to post on social media. It's easy to look like change. But the only way to leave a true legacy and impact is to be the change. That's why I'm always telling my followers, "Live it. Breathe it. Be it." Somebody, somewhere, at some time is watching what you do. You're an inspiration, whether you want the title or not. You're inspiring people in either a positive way or a negative one. So, what does your life say? Not your words, but your *life*!

Receiving a great legacy is a truly remarkable gift. I was fortunate enough to grow up in a family with supportive and ambitious parents who always made me believe that I could do and be whatever I wanted. That was an amazing legacy, and it put me firmly on the path to being the person I've become. And their legacy was especially important when things weren't going well for me. Remember: life is always going to throw challenges at you, and being provided with a great legacy can't shield you from all of them. But what it can do is give you better internal resources. When things were darkest for me, I had the legacy of my parents to fall back on, to remind me that I was strong and capable—and that surrendering to the darkness was not something I was meant to do. I was supposed to build on the legacy that had been left for me and keep making it greater.

You see, it isn't only the negative cycles that keep repeating themselves. The positive cycles work the same way. That's why people who grow up in secure families tend to raise their kids in a secure family. It's why successful people raise successful kids. It's why people who fight to make the best of their lives inspire their children (or their nieces and nephews, or the people in their communities) to do everything they can to make the best of their own lives. When you leave a great legacy, you give others an amazing gift—you give them a huge lead when they take the baton from you. And if part of your legacy is that you had to overcome enormous troubles or maybe get beyond the negative legacy that was left for you, that's even better, because you're not just leaving a legacy of accomplishment but a legacy that shows it's possible to get beyond difficult circumstances and still have a great life.

And these things build on each other. The legacy you leave to the next generation could be the foundation on which even greater legacies are built. That's what the Tupac quote at the start of this section is all about. You may not change the world, but your legacy could be the thing that leads others to change the world. As I said, you're touching lives all the time. If you touch them in a positive way, you're perpetuating a cycle that could lead to amazing things.

You're Already on Your Way to Creating a Great Legacy

Okay, so I've convinced you that you want to leave a great legacy. But how do you make sure that you do it? Well, that's really what we've been talking about since the beginning of this book.

When you stop running away from your battles, you face up to the roadblocks that have been preventing you from being the best version of yourself. Instead of trying to stay one step ahead of your troubles, you turn around, face them, and do the hard work necessary to end them. You have those tools now, and a person who doesn't run from his or her most important battles is going to leave an extremely valuable legacy.

When you figure out what your purpose is and you start building your life to allow you to live that purpose, you're operating on a much higher level than you ever could if you went through life without purpose. People who are living their purpose send the message that life is about a whole lot more than running out the clock. That's a great legacy to pass along, and you know how to discover your purpose now.

When you come to accept that your story can still end well even if it has some bad chapters, you're taking control of your situation and taking the steps necessary to put an end to the bad part of your story and become the hero. Rather than having the hard stuff in your life define you, you turn those things into the "interesting" part of your story that makes your triumph that much sweeter. When you leave a legacy of resilience and perseverance, you're leaving behind something that absolutely everyone needs.

When you make the painful decision to burn all of the bridges that don't lead you to being the greatest you, you're cutting yourself off from the destructive behaviors that have been holding you back. You've faced up to the reality of where those bridges were leading you, and you've decided that you can't go there anymore. If your legacy includes stories of tough choices that had to be made to keep you on your journey, it serves as a model for others when they inevitably contend with circumstances that aren't healthy for them.

When you make yet another painful decision, this time to dig up all of the bad seeds that have been planted around you, you're eliminating the people in your life who—intentionally or not—are doing you harm. You're making the distinction between those who are good for you and those who might make you feel good in the moment but ultimately keep you from being the greatest you. This is another priceless legacy because you're showing future generations that short-term pain is sometimes necessary for long-term gain and that this is almost always the best choice.

When you come to understand that the true beneficiary of forgiveness is not those you forgive but yourself, you give yourself two invaluable gifts: the gift of peace and the gift of freedom. By finally forgiving, you are no longer reliving the terrible things that have been done against you; you're moving on from them instead. And when you forgive, you finally grant yourself the freedom to conduct the rest of your life without being haunted by your past. This is an amazingly valuable legacy to leave to others because if they can understand the importance of forgiveness at a young age, they won't ever have to bear the burden of holding grudges.

When you take the important steps to protect your peace, you give yourself the tools necessary to head into your day with the best chance of a positive outcome. Instead of starting your day with things that clutter your mind and leave you on the defensive, you begin with something that uplifts you, inspires you, and brings you a tiny bit of joy. If part of your legacy is that you made sure to first protect your peace before going out into the world, you're modeling the value of this for all who come after you.

When you adopt the championship mind-set, you're convincing yourself that good enough isn't good enough for you, and you're practicing the traits that will prepare you to act like a winner at every important stage in your life. You're acknowledging that improvement and striving for perfection isn't something that you do for a couple of weeks every year, but something you commit to on an ongoing basis. If future generations get that from you and just naturally operate this way, they'll be thanking you forever.

And when you acknowledge that your relationship is your world and that you need to commit yourself to being a great partner, you're providing yourself with the best chance of having a sturdy foundation throughout your life. You're creating a safe space for yourself and those you love, and you're making your own world the most important world in the universe. That's a wonderful legacy to leave, and leaving it is in many ways part of doing it in the first place. When you establish this example of "home," whatever home might be, you're showing others how to get their priorities right.

And when you add all of these up, you provide the most important legacy of all: the greatest you. You show everyone who matters to you, everyone who might someday matter to you, and the people who will someday matter to them, that doing the work necessary to be the best version of yourself is a noble endeavor that will resonate far into the future.

And this, at last, is your higher cause. Being the greatest you will take you from wherever you were when you started this book to a place filled with purpose, connection, and fulfillment. And if that's not amazing enough, it will also leave a legacy that you can be proud of leaving and that will benefit so many others for generations to come.

I hope you understand now that all of this is achievable, no matter where you were when you started this book. Some of the steps you take might be very difficult for you, but I'm convinced they will all be extremely rewarding. If your life has been especially tough, getting through these steps might take longer, and you might even need to revisit a few of them. But if you stick with it, I am completely sure that you're going to discover the best version of yourself, the version you were meant to be.

Congratulations on getting to this point. You're going to love being the greatest you. As I tell my followers at the end of every single message, it all starts with you.

It's RehabTime.

Let's get it.

ACKNOWLEDGMENTS

Thank you to:

Maria, Tristan, Maya, George, Aqua, Todd, and Terry
Shelton, my family.
Lou Aronica, my writer.
Scott Houffman, my agent.
Brenda Cardenas, my executive assistant.
Shane Connelly, my executive producer.
Ryan Sprague, my cover designer
Jason Suarez, my photographer.
Dean Graziosi, my mentor.
The team at Nelson Books: Webster Younce, Brigitta
Nortker, Karen Jackson, and Sara Broun.

ABOUT THE AUTHORS

Trent Shelton is a former NFL wide receiver who is now considered one of the most impactful speakers of this generation. He reaches more than 50 million people weekly through his various social media outlets and travels the world to speak his message of creating lasting change in your life. Trent and his wife, Maria, live in Fort Worth, Texas, with their two children, Tristan and Maya. It's RehabTime, let's get it!

Lou Aronica is the *New York Times* bestselling author of more than two dozen books, including the nonfiction works *The Element* (with Sir Ken Robinson) and *The Culture Code* (with Dr. Clotaire Rapaille) and the novels *The Forever Year* and *Blue*.